Happily
Even
After

BY ALAN COHEN

Books

Are You As Happy As Your Dog?
Dare to Be Yourself
A Deep Breath of Life
The Dragon Doesn't Live Here Anymore*
Handle with Prayer*
Have You Hugged a Monster Today?
I Had It All the Time*
Joy Is My Compass
Lifestyles of the Rich in Spirit
The Peace That You Seek
Rising in Love
Setting the Seen

* Also available as an audio book

Audiocassettes

Deep Relaxation
Eden Morning
I Believe in You
Journey to the Center of the Heart (also a CD)
Living from the Heart
Peace

Videocassette

Wisdom of the Spirit

(All of the above are available through Alan Cohen Publications:
800-462-3013 or
Hay House, Inc.: 800-654-5126.)

Please visit the Hay House Website at: **www.hayhouse.com** and
Alan Cohen's Website at: **www.alancohen.com**

Happily
Even
After

Can You Be Friends After Lovers?

Alan Cohen

HAY
HOUSE

Hay House, Inc.
Carlsbad, CA

Editorial: Jill Kramer   *Design:* Renée G. Noël

The material in the book is directed toward individuals or couples who have already divorced or separated, or who are in the process of doing so. The intention of this work is to offer such readers wisdom, inspiration, and techniques to create a happier and healthier relationship with their former partners. This book is in no way intended to encourage any reader to leave a marriage or relationship prematurely or irresponsibly. Any reader considering leaving a marriage or relationship should engage in personal introspection and/or seek the advice of a counselor or qualified professional before doing so.

All of the stories in this book are true. To honor the privacy of the writers and their former partners, most of the names have been changed, as well as some minor identifying details.

Note to readers: In the interest of gender sensitivity, the author alternates between the use of male and female pronouns throughout the book.

Library of Congress Cataloging-in-Publication Data

Cohen, Alan.
      Happily even after : can you be friends after lovers? / Alan Cohen.
         p.   cm.
      ISBN 1-56170-629-9 (trade pbk.)
      1. Divorce–Psychological aspects.   2. Divorced people–
psychology.   3. Man-woman relationships.   I. Title.
HQ814.C64   1999
306.89–dc21
                                           99-27904
                                           CIP

ISBN 1-56170-629-9

02 01 00 99   4 3 2 1
First Printing, August 1999

Printed in the United States of America

To the couples who believe in love,
with deep appreciation for those
who have shared their stories here.

&❧ Contents ❧&

*"The holiest spot on earth
is where an ancient hatred
has become a present love."*

— A Course in Miracles

Introduction

While driving through San Francisco late one night, I happened upon a radio station that played songs requested by callers. A young woman named Carol asked that a particular song be played for a fellow named Eddie.

"And who is Eddie?" asked the DJ, a mature woman with a sultry voice perfectly suited for late-night radio and romance.

"Eddie is my husband," the caller answered, "actually, my soon-to-be ex-husband—he's leaving our marriage."

"Then why would you want to dedicate a song to him?" the DJ retorted, her voice abruptly shifting from seductress to intimidator.

"Because I want him to be happy, and I want to stay friends with him always."

"You want to stay friends with a guy who ruined your life?"

"He didn't ruin my life," Carol answered firmly. "We had a lot of wonderful times together, and even though we are going our separate ways, we care about each other. That's why I'm dedicating this song to him."

"Oh, all right," the DJ answered with a sigh of surrender. The song began to play.

As I made my way along Route 101 in the quiet of the night, it occurred to me that this conversation symbolized two very different approaches to relationship: one that has dominated our culture for as long as I can remember, and one that feels new and even radical. The old way is based on the belief that when a relationship ends, it was a failure because it did not turn into a marriage or the marriage did not fulfill its "until death do us part" vow. One person is cast as a villain, and the other a victim. Blame is hurled back and forth until the two people—who once adored each other—turn their backs on one another, or one person pines endlessly for his or her lost soulmate. If the couple divorces, brutal warfare ensues over property settlements, alimony, and child custody. Then both people go on to create the same relationship with the next partner, who promises to be different but turns out to be the same, or is different but just as bad or worse. Meanwhile, both partners struggle to pick up the pieces of their broken lives, and perhaps enter therapy to try to figure out, "Why am I so screwed up?"

Can this really be the way we were meant to live? Must heartbreak and enmity be the natural end products of love? Or is there another way in which we can approach relationship parting that bestows us with strength and empowerment rather than pain and sadness?

Yes, there is. The way in which Carol chose to end her relationship is called "Big Love." The purpose of a Big Love relationship is to open, learn, grow, discover more about who we are, enjoy the unique riches we bring to each other, and expand as spiritual beings. Big Love defines the success of a relationship not by the weight of the diamond in an engagement ring or how long the marriage lasts, but by the quality of aliveness we experience while the relationship thrives. Big Love recognizes that how we part is as important as how we were together; that love and harmony are more important than being right; and that mutual support is more vital than sex, romance, or even staying together. Big Love acknowledges that our happiness does not hinge on the actions of another person, but proceeds from a Source deep inside us. No matter what a mate does for or against us, we always have the power to choose love—perhaps not always the romantic love that we were taught to pursue, but a higher and greater spiritual love that endures forever.

Those who practice Big Love understand one crucial principle that is painfully absent in its more popular yet more limiting relative, shaky love: *The key to enjoying a better relationship with your next partner is to find healing and completion with the last one,* and to appreciate both the joys you shared and what you learned through the challenges. Unless you have come to greater self-understanding through your last relationship, you will most likely repeat it the next time around. Then you'll wring your hands and shout to the universe, "Why is this happening to me again?" Sooner or later it becomes obvious that we do not attract relationship partners by chance. Who shows up depends on who we are, and who we are depends on what we've learned from who we've been. Before we can expand, we must heal.

Happily Even After brings Big Love to life and focuses in detail on what it takes to move from fear and separateness to mutual empowerment. If you are ready to grow beyond struggle, this book offers you a new vision and many tools to live it. In the pages to come, you will meet more than two dozen couples who have found creative ways to love themselves and their former mates, and who have moved on to more satisfying relationships with their exes and, eventually, their new partners. They are real people, just like you and me, who in some cases ascended from the deepest dregs of bitterness and resentment and chose to get on with their lives by cultivating honest appreciation.

I hold three powerful intentions for you as you set out on your adventure through these principles and stories. I envision that you will: (1) find deeper healing, peace, and win-win solutions to the issues that have challenged you in your past relationships; (2) open the door for brighter and more nourishing energy with your next partner; and—most important—(3) learn to love, honor, and cherish yourself in the process—so deeply that there is no doubt in your mind that you're worthy of having the relationships your heart truly desires.

— *Alan Cohen*

c h a p t e r   1

Husbands for Dinner

Excellent Exes

*"Forgiveness does not change the past, but it
does enlarge the future."*

— Paul Boese

"On Father's Day, I took my two ex-husbands out to dinner," Danielle told me nonchalantly.

"Excuse me?"

"Why not?" she countered. "Steve and Randy are the two most important men in my life; they are the fathers of my children, and we are all connected. I wanted to honor them for the good they have brought into my world."

My immediate reactions were: (1) *Are you serious?* and (2) *We could make a mint by selling this story as a sitcom.* But then as I sat and digested my friend's account, I began to like what I'd heard. The more I thought about it, the more I respected Danielle for keeping her former mates in her heart and acknowledging their importance in her life.

Let's face it: Danielle's dinner is an exception to the way you and I were taught to deal with the end of relationships. In a million obvious and subtle ways, our culture has taught us that when a relationship is over, both parties go their separate ways, and at least one is hurt and upset. One person is a creep for leaving, and the other is left out in the cold. I can envision a *Seinfeld* episode in which George grills Jerry during a postmortem of a recent breakup: "Were you the *dumper* or the *dumpee?*"

We do not have to dig very deep to discover the source of our programmed attitudes. Countless pop-song lyrics, novel plots, and romantic movie themes have glorified and capitalized on the villain/victim model.

While many of us were weaned on co-dependent Weepy-Waily Victim Songs, few of us have taken the time to step back and ask, "Is there an option other than the one I've been shown? Am I doomed to live out the rest of my life feeling separate from those I once cared for deeply? Is there a way I can remain friends with my ex and feel good about him or her, as well as myself?"

It is not only possible to enjoy a lasting and rewarding relationship with your ex; it is *inevitable*, for two reasons:

1. Once we are in relationship, we are in relationship forever.
2. All enmity must eventually give way to healing.

"But," you may sincerely contend, "you don't know about *my* relationship—I don't ever want to see that horrible jerk again, let alone be friends."

You don't need to ever see that "horrible jerk" again, but *for your own well-being,* you need to come to perceive the relationship in a way that will empower you so you won't feel drained and emotionally poisoned every time you think of your former partner. No matter what he or she is doing or feeling, you must find a way out of pain and anger *for your own peace of mind.*

You cannot get on with creating better future relationships unless you come to terms with past ones; otherwise, life is just one long *Groundhog Day* in which you keep attracting the same kind of partner—different actor, same story. Are you ready to write a new script with a more satisfying ending?

You don't deserve to live in pain, fear, or resentment, and you don't need to. In spite of what we have been taught and experienced . . .

We can create our partings in any way we choose.

Rather than storming away in a cloud of resentment, you can use your experience to build what could be one of the greatest friendships of a lifetime, and become a springboard to healthier and happier relationships in all aspects of your life.

Even if your relationship did not have a happy *ending, you can have a* healthy *ending.* More and more couples are deciding that being in harmony is more important than being right. As a culture, we are participating in an all-important cultural shift from torturous endings to more soul-satisfying connections. We are paving the way for relationship completions that add to the quality of our lives, rather than destroying them. There is hope for all relationships, including yours. Nothing is so botched up that it cannot be restored to kindness and dignity through sincerity, caring, and love. Are you open to a greater possibility for love, starting now? Read Sally and Joseph's inspiring relationship story.

Here is how one couple found their deeper connection:

∽∽

Cielle and Robert:
The Relationship Didn't Die;
It Changed for the Better

Six years ago, I broke up a marriage of 18 years. My husband, Robert, and I had three children. All of us were unhappy in the family we had created. We were immersed in worry, anger, fear, withdrawal, resentment, and victimization, while pretending to be a perfect and happy family. I left the marriage when I began to see how unhappy we all were. The rest of my family, however, was not ready to acknowledge this truth. They were hor-

rified by what I did, viewing me as the insane enemy tearing apart family unity. I, as the mother and wife who had been the nourisher and comforter, was now the destroyer, not to be trusted. The pain and shock were nearly unbearable. Our unhappy but predictable status quo became a nightmare of uncertainty, as any sense of stability was pulled away.

The marriage did not survive, but the family did heal. Each of us is much stronger and healthier emotionally, which is expressed in greater creativity, honesty, self-acceptance, happiness, and depth of emotion.

One of the first strokes of good fortune after our breakup came at a Thanksgiving family gathering where my brother attended with both his first wife and his second wife of several years. It was a true inspiration for me to see them all together enjoying each other's company. Their friendship had developed as a result of their commitment to give the best care to their son. Both mom and stepmom joined in partnership rather than competition, to help raise the boy between two families. The mutual dedication to give the best of themselves to the boy created a true bond of friendship between my brother, his wife, and his former wife. Seeing this concrete vision of what could be, I wanted to create a similar situation in my own life. I decided to strive for a state of friendship and cooperation with Joseph and any significant others that might come into his life.

Robert and I spent five years moving from separation to divorce; we were not in a rush. We took the time to make sure that every issue in our divorce decree was something that we both felt good about. We used both counselors and mediators to help us come to a settlement, but we didn't use lawyers. We did not want to create the antagonistic mind-set of one party suing the other for wrongdoing. We considered this a matter of the heart, and we wanted to both "win."

Robert and I decided that although we had irreconcilable differences as husband and wife, we were both dedicated to raising our children. Whenever we had a disagreement regarding our *settlement, we chose to look at the situation—from the visitation schedule to who would keep the couch—from the standpoint of what would be best for the kids. This gave us a common focus, a platform for cooperation. In time, we developed a partnership based on cooperation and respect.*

One unique living arrangement that we have used for five and a half years is that our children continue to live in our family home. Robert and I move in and out of the house to care for them. This has given our children a sense of stability, predictability, and power, while building a sense of cooperation between Joseph and me. Some people have been surprised that we have been able to sustain this arrangement for so many years, yet my family is much happier now than we were before the breakup.

My former husband and I have built a new relationship based on friendship and trust. I admire him immensely for the life he leads, and I've learned that it's okay to nurture a different relationship than the one we had in the past. The relationship didn't die; it changed—and it changed for the better!

chapter 2

Learners and Losers

Growing Beyond Victim

*"Americans, who make more of marrying for love than any other
people, also break up more of their marriages, but the figure
reflects not so much the failure of love as the determination
not to live without it."*

— Morton Hunt

My friend Andrea is a popular college instructor of human
relations, and a relationship counselor. She has also been
married four times, and divorced three. At a party we
both attended, I overheard one of Andrea's former students ask
her, "How can you pass yourself off as a relationship expert when
you are a four-time loser?"

Andrea responded coolly, "I don't see myself as a four-time
loser; I consider myself a four-time *learner*. Although those marriages didn't endure, I gained valuable lessons that helped me
bring more depth and presence to the relationships that followed,
and ultimately contributed to the successful marriage I now have."

If you feel like a loser because your marriage or relationship
has ended, re-identify yourself as a learner.

If you are wiser for your experience, it was a success.

Rather than criticizing yourself for your shortcomings, honor yourself for the courage to grow through experience.

As evolving beings, we discover what works by evaluating the results of what didn't work; we grow as much (usually more) through our errors as we do through our successes. Like a child learning to ride a bicycle, the information we gain from falling is just as valuable as the feedback we get from staying balanced. Every attempt, whether a "success" or "failure," ultimately contributes to our skill. Seen in this way, we are *always* progressing toward our goal.

One of the most difficult and painful questions to answer is, *"Why did your relationship fail?"* When faced with such an inquiry, remember that *ending* is not the same as *failure*. Your relationship would be a failure only if you did not learn from it. If you gained insight, self-awareness, or strength, and you would choose more wisely next time, you are significantly ahead of where you began.

Begin to *reframe* your past relationships as successful learning experiences.

We form new relationships according to the way
we think about our old ones.

If you dwell on your past failures, you will manufacture new ones. Focus on what you gained from past relationships, and you will build a foundation for success in your new ones.

Here are some criteria by which losers are distinguished from learners:

Loser	**Learner**
Denies sense of sorrow, grief, or loss	Acknowledges pain without indulging it
Blames partner for failure	Inventories own actions
Criticizes self for failure	Honors self for willingness to learn
Plunges into self-pity	Explores self-awareness
Forms judgments about opposite sex	Gathers information to ensure future success
Seeks agreement from "allies" to bolster victim position	Turns to friends for support to keep mind and heart open
Turns to favored addiction to numb pain	Turns to Higher Power to grow beyond pain
Seeks new relationship immediately to offset sense of loss	Takes time to get reacquainted with self and integrate experience
Revels in ex-partner's pain or guilt	Delights in ex-partner's well-being
Seeks to punish ex-partner	Offers kindness and support to ex-partner
Seeks retribution	Lets go and gets on with life

BEYOND KEN AND BARBIE

Many "model" couples live picture-perfect marriages with fine homes in the suburbs, well-paying jobs, several expensive automobiles, and bright children who make the honor roll. Behind the scenes, however, many such marriages are devoid of intimacy, communication, and growth. In my seminars, I have heard a significant number of divorced men and women confess, "We looked great on the outside, but I was dying on the inside." Just because a couple fulfills societal expectations for a model marriage, it doesn't mean that they are achieving their deeper purpose of growing as individuals. Someone who becomes stronger and more self-aware through a painful divorce, by contrast, accomplishes more for his or her spiritual growth than one who sleepwalks through a lifeless marriage.

Do not be deceived by appearances, and do not allow yourself to fall prey to the belief that you are here to live up to the expectations of others.

Your life is valuable not for how it looks,
but for what is happening in your heart and soul.

If a relationship falls apart in the outer world, but you extract personal growth from it, you are succeeding in a far more meaningful way than one who amasses the symbols of success but fails to recognize his or her own *inner* worth. The only true measure of success, we eventually discover, is happiness.

After my book *The Dragon Doesn't Live Here Anymore* was published, I received a telephone call from a nun inviting me to present a seminar to the Catholic ministry for the divorced and separated. Sister Alice explained that many Catholics felt angry and guilty about their crashed marriages, and then she asked me what I titled my workshop. Laughing, I told her, "I usually call it 'The Dragon Doesn't Live Here Anymore,' but in this case I think we should use another title."

I found that the greatest need of the participants in the divorced and separated ministry was *self-forgiveness*. While these people struggled with tremendous pain and grief in the wake of their broken relationships, they shouldered the added burden of condemnation from the church, which defined them as sinners for ending their marriages. Their lives were difficult enough, I surmised, without having to bear the stigma of excommunication. These folks did not need to worry about going to hell—they were already there!

The divorced women and men in this group demonstrated great courage in leaving their marriages in the face of the ecclesiastical judgment they faced. They needed to find compassion for themselves and forgiveness for their mates. I honored the church for establishing a ministry to support this segment of their parishioners. In the long run, these people grew a great deal from facing and overcoming their fears, and they gained strength that they may not have found if they had remained in barren marriages.

BROKEN OPEN

If you have been closed or armored, a painful breakup can lead you to rediscover yourself and open to a depth of aliveness you might never have known if you had just coasted along in your comfort zone.

If your heart has been broken, let it be broken open.

Opportunities Bestowed by a Broken Heart

Get in touch with your feelings

Reach out for support

Appreciate the love of friends

Gain insight into the patterns that have run your life

Tell more truth about who you are and what you want

Claim your power to establish your own destiny

Express creativity (poetry, music, art, original expression)

Discover and develop a relationship with your spiritual source

Deepen in compassion

Make changes in your life that you might not have otherwise made

Learn how to find richer rewards in your next relationship

The voice of shaky love tells you that your relationship ending has ruined your life, while Big Love whispers that you now have more life available to you. The road through hell leads to the door of heaven. So your breakup merits not bitterness or resentment, but gratitude and appreciation.

Popular singer Kenny Loggins went through a major crisis when his marriage ended. As he searched his soul to discover his truth and explain his divorce to his children, he found within himself a deeper strength and love. This process moved him so profoundly that he wrote many passionate and heartfelt songs about his insights, and collected them into an album called *Leap of Faith,* which went on to become one of his most successful productions. Many listeners remark that the honesty and vulnerability Kenny displayed in these songs helped them through similarly challenging times. (Since that time, Kenny has remarried, and he and his new wife Julia have intimately chronicled their love and marriage in a most inspiring book and album, *The Unimaginable Life.*[1])

Similarly, when Native American descendant William Least Heat-Moon lost his job and his wife left him, he plunged into deep introspection. In the process of attempting to rebuild his broken life, William recalled his dream to explore the country. Free and unencumbered, he bought a Volkswagen van and sat down to plan his route. As he surveyed the map, William noticed that the major thoroughfares were indicated with thick red lines, while the smaller byways and country roads were marked by thinner blue lines. William realized that he wanted an adventure, and decided to travel the side roads. On his trek, he interacted with fascinating people, received many insights he would never have discovered in his old routine, and reconnected with his Native American heritage. After his two-year odyssey, William had filled his journal with a wealth of colorful stories, and he had them published. *Blue Highways*[2] went on to become a national bestseller, and William Least Heat-Moon was catapulted into an entirely more meaningful world. Although he could not see the plan in the midst of his hardship, his breakup launched him into the life he had always dreamed of.

THE FAST-FORWARD AGE

We are living in a time of accelerated learning. Many people now go through two, three, or more marriages in a lifetime, and participate in many more relationships. We may have judged ourselves harshly for having several mates or numerous relationships, and we may believe that there is something wrong with us for failing the societal expectation of staying with one person for a lifetime.

But . . .

What happens to you is not as important as what you make of it.

To find peace, reframe your opinion of how you or life "should" be. You are, and have been, on your right path.

> *What you thought was **wrong** with you*
> *may be what is **right** with you.*

In wisdom you chose to go through a number of significant relationships so you could master many lessons in a short period of time.

> *You have not missed your destiny;*
> *you are in the process of fulfilling it.*

If you lived in an earlier century, your relationships would have told quite a different story and brought you very different lessons. You would have married one person for a lifetime, lived in one town, worked in one vocation, attended one church, and adopted one belief system. Your life would have been slower and simpler—as would your learning. In those days, it might have taken you an entire lifetime to master the lessons of a relationship with a particular person.

Now, the pace and purpose of our relationships is different. Rather than marrying for survival, economic, social, or political expedience—and being assigned to a spouse by your parents, priest, or an astrologer—we marry for love, romance, companionship, communication, sexual expression, and spiritual growth—of our own free will. These higher ideals and increased levels of personal responsibility call forth all kinds of issues that marrying for survival never touched on. In greater soul maturity, we have taken on deeper, richer, more subtle, and more varied lessons. In accordance with our curriculum, our life changes call us to face our fears, confront our unconsciousness, and bring light to the shadow selves we have chosen to master.

Several marriages or many relationships in a lifetime are not necessarily signs of weakness; they may be an indication of your dedication to discover greater truths about who you are and what you are here to do. If, at the end of your life, you are a wiser person for your relationship experiences, they have all been worth it. And . . .

If you have learned to love,
you have fulfilled your highest purpose.

No matter how many relationships you have gone through, marriages you have ended, or mistakes you have made, *never define yourself as a loser*. Instead, be grateful for the awareness you have gained, and be proud of yourself for your bravery in learning by doing. Recognize that you are not the person you were 20 years, or even 20 days, ago. Remember that the Big Picture is unfolding perfectly even if you do not see it in a given moment.

Real learning usually occurs gradually—rarely overnight. You are always adding to your wisdom. When you disown your identity as a loser and adopt that of a learner, you are on your way to being a master. One day you will discover that everything that has happened to you has been an element in your awakening to the beauty in you and around you. Then you will be able to bless all experiences and honor everyone who assisted you to grow.

∽∽
Diana and Carey:
I Am Spiritual; I Am Strong

I was 24 when I met Carey, and 26 when I married him. Those two years were tumultuous—abusive at the very least, and certainly dysfunctional. He was an alcoholic, and I was co-dependent. I had no conscious knowledge of this at the beginning—I had never really been aware of these labels applying to me or my personal life. Oh, sure, we both had family members who were alcoholic, but this dysfunction really didn't apply to us. I gained more than 100 pounds while dating this man, and during the marriage he informed me that he had a problem with that. There always seemed to be something wrong with me. I wasn't so bad as long as I was his cheerleader and partner in complaining about the world, ripping apart our family members, or sitting back and bemoaning how life had done him wrong. We were hate buddies, and I was drowning in the muck of negativity.

Looking back, I see that the teachers in my life were lining up to assist me on my journey. As I started going to Overeaters Anonymous, I became aware of self-defeating behavior, yet my husband's verbal abuse accelerated and was unyielding when it came to how I cooked, what I spent, who my friends were, where I went, the books I was reading, how I kept the house, and more. Then a number of human "angels" showed up to open doors of awareness for me. My feet needed to move into action, my mind needed to create a healthier emotional environment, and my heart needed to heal. And so each day became a new journey. I worked on my issues, built a spiritual network of supportive friends, amended my past, and dreamed of my true bliss. In fact, I was encouraged to dream—not just in my head, but by doing something tangible. So I began journaling, masterminding, treasure-mapping, and allowing myself to become my honored guest in my life.

It takes whatever it takes for however long it takes. I stayed in the abuse and neglect—the months and years of no touching, sex, or affection. I received all my love and light from 12-step program peers, church folks, community activities, school, and work. Basically, I got my strokes from everyone outside of my home. My hope was that one day I could believe in what they saw in me more than what I believed about myself.

For years I had bought the lies about my lack of worth. I had no idea of my value to myself or others, and I thought I had no impact on people. I wrote much and often. I participated in writing workshops, inner child exploration, and spiritual retreats. I immersed myself in New Thought tapes, sermons, Native American spirituality, self-help books, New Age music, crystals, smudging, and affirmations, and I put my family and friends through hell as I metamorphosed into a cutting-edge evolving woman. I got involved in service to my community, my church, and my recovery programs.

The crucial point came when the pain of staying became worse than the fear of leaving. All the footwork and action steps that I had taken were being called forth—put up or shut up. My inner voice called, "Helloooooooooooo? If you think it's about sitting on your backside and reading, meditating, and getting it from someone else through osmosis, think again!" I realized that if I was going to make real change, I would have to act. It took all those studies and things to fill me, to wake me up, to show me how. Then one day God said, "Walk, little girl," and it had to be my feet. Those activities were my tools for building and my teachers for new possibilities.

The Sunday messages at my progressive church continued to open my eyes to dreaming, seeing, and believing that I could manifest a new and better life. I had learned that if it's gonna be, it's up to me, that I must make my changes from a position of love or I will be destined to repeat them. I knew that I did not want a repeat of my past ten years—or anything prior. So I began loving myself out of my marriage. I continually was reminded that "this is going to be the best year of my life . . . without exception." And it was.

When I told my husband I was leaving, I said, "It's not because I don't love you; it's because I love me more." This is one of the strongest statements I have ever made. It took three other women and 45 minutes to get me moved out of my home, while very loving parents, sisters and their families, and a whole lot of dear friends supported me after that. I kept my life very simple while I worked days as a word processing specialist and evenings and weekends as a licensed massage therapist.

For the next seven months, I was in a fog. How I functioned was truly by the grace of God; it was a spiritual journey. The first year of separation from my husband was nothing compared to the years of separation between myself and God. It was about opening my arms and allowing myself to be consciously aware of God in my life. God was always there, but I had let the world drama be the first priority, and there were no other positions. I continued my growth by going off to a 28-day life recovery program, which propelled me into a completely new dimension of my absolute best. When the student is ready, the teacher appears. *Now my priorities are God first, myself second, and others third.*

Life as I knew it had changed to such a degree that the future I had dreamed about, wrote about, prayed about, affirmed, and desired no longer existed just in my mind—it was my life; it was my present day.

Since that turning point, I have discovered that I have many gifts and talents I was not aware of. I am a writer, singer, success-

17

ful artist, workshop facilitator, mentor, healer, passionate lover, dynamic and bliss-filled woman, and a channel for God's energy to flow through on a daily basis.

Now I realize that it is trust and faith and courage and risk and action and dreaming and knowing and honoring and gratitude—all of it, not just one thing. Yet sometimes at midnight when there are no friends and family close by, and I'm in my bed alone and my guts feel like they're hanging out and I can't stop crying, it's about my relationship with my Higher Power and where God is in my life. I'm not a religious woman; I am a spiritual woman, a strong woman.

c h a p t e r　3

Until Life Do Us Join

Good-bye to Guilt

"When two people are under the influence of the most violent, most insane, most delusive, and most transient of passions, they are required to swear that they will remain in that excited, abnormal, and exhausting condition continuously until death do them part."
— George Bernard Shaw

Until *death do us part* is by far the most formidable vow that comes back to haunt us at the time of divorce. You and your mate promised true love for a lifetime, and here you are a year, ten, or 30 later declaring, "I can't do this." You meant the vow when you uttered it, but now you feel like a hypocrite, fool, or failure. Is there any way to come to terms with making such a big promise that you were unable to keep?

There is. "Until death do us part" applies not only to the body, but to relationships as well. Because you are a spiritual being, it is the state of your *spirit* that determines how alive or dead you are. The death of a relationship is just as real as the death of a body—sometimes more so. If a relationship is dead, there is no purpose in keeping the two bodies together. Just because two bodies live under one roof and sleep in the same bed does not mean they are married. And just because two bodies are not in the same place does not mean they are separate. We all know couples who stay together for a lifetime but live worlds apart, while other couples are geographically distant but united in spirit. In relationship . . .

The state of the art is the state of the heart.

There are two primary reasons relationships come to an organic death: The first is that *the couple got together for the wrong reasons.*

Wrong Reasons for Couples Getting Together

Massive illusions about who the other person is ✓

Loneliness or a sense of personal inadequacy

Sheer sexual passion

Romantic fantasy ✓

Rebounding from the last disaster

Pressure from partner, family, peers, religion, or society

To snub family, religion, peers, or society

To get back at the last partner

Pregnancy without commitment

Sense of indebtedness ("He helped me through a hard time")

Fear of turning 30, 40, or 50 and looking like a loser

Fear of growing old and not having someone

Desire for a handyman, housekeeper, or child-care provider

Marrying his potential while overlooking his reality

"She will save me from the hardships of my life"

"I will save him from the hardships of his life"
Financial security
To keep him/her from straying or leaving

If an individual or a couple makes a poor choice in unconsciousness to get married at a young (or any) age for the wrong reasons, must they suffer for a lifetime? Only a sadist would suggest that someone pay for a mistake for eternity. Shaky love, ever motivated by fear, urges, "Hold on to what you have. You may be miserable, but this is better than nothing or the unknown." Big Love, on the other hand, teaches that if you recognize you have made a mistake you can't rectify, you only serve to acknowledge it and then move on, bolstered by the experience that will prevent you from repeating it. Sometimes the greatest act of love a couple can perform is to admit that what was, is no more, or perhaps never was at all. While such a decision is always painful to consider, the courage to face and act on it is immensely liberating, and often draws a couple closer than they ever were in a situation that did not befit them.

If a relationship has died in spirit and you exert fruitless effort to keep the corpse animated, you will be hard-pressed to find energy for creativity or expansion. (The hilarious movie *Weekend at Bernie's* recounts the tale of two young men who find their boss's corpse, and to avoid being considered murder suspects, carry his body through a weekend of social activities, keeping him propped up through hysterical situations.) If you find that the majority of your energy is tied up in processing your relationship or trying to present a healthy front for a sick situation, you may qualify for the *Weekend at Bernie's* "Can't Make a Dead Horse Whinny" award. In such a case, you have no choice but to confront your issues and agree that you need to do something different. You can either dive into the relationship and do what it takes to restore it to (perhaps greater) health, or leave before it kills both of you. Either choice is much kinder and more empowering than dragging the carcass around.

The second primary reason that relationships die is that *the individuals have grown in different directions*. While you started out with common interests in Metallica, smoking pot, and watching *Beavis and Butthead* at some point you set out on a spiritual path and felt drawn to a new lifestyle. You invited your husband to join you, but he just wasn't interested. You tried and tried to involve him in your life, and you tried to take an interest in his, but as time moved on, you felt as if you were sitting in the same theater but watching different movies. Although you still slept and ate under the same roof, your heart called you to a lifestyle based on different values. Then you distracted yourself with busyness to override the aching of your heart. Or you got bogged down in your daily routine. Or you ate compulsively. Or one of you had an affair to try to offset the emptiness. Or you just resigned yourself to the thought that it must be God's will for you to somehow fulfill yourself in other ways. Then you died a little bit every day, acting as if everything was fine, but inside knowing that there had to be more.

But if you are not growing in a relationship (as in all of life), you are dying. The notion of things staying the same is an illusion; the more fixed your roles become, the more your souls shrivel. The purpose of relationship is to expand in dynamic aliveness, greeting each new day and moment as a blessed opportunity for joyful discovery of self, partner, and life. The attraction to regularity, on the other hand, is a trick of the mind to convince you that the status quo offers security rather than embalming.

As dynamic beings, we are always evolving. Sometimes we learn and grow side by side, and sometimes our paths diverge. It is neither a sin nor a tragedy when two people's interests do not line up anymore; it just *is*. To try to make believe that you are the people you were ten years ago is to deny whom you have become. If you have grown deeper and closer, that is a great blessing. If you have grown apart, you must tell the truth about it.

Couples who part as a result of divergent paths do not have to find fault or blame anyone. No one is wrong; both of you are right for being who and where you are; in fact, both of you are to be commended for being true to yourselves. No one has the right to sit in judgment and say, "My path is better than yours." If you and your partner are both true to your individual paths, you are living in integrity. We can fully acknowledge our differences while loving, honoring, and respecting each other. If you can stay with integrity, your souls will knit in the most meaningful way. And if you can part in integrity, you lay the foundation for your next right step.

There is a third reason that relationships die, but it is not organic, and it is not truly a death. If one person in the couple becomes afraid and leaves because his fear of intimacy outweighs his desire to be fully present in the relationship, the relationship hits a wall and cannot grow. In such a case, however, the story is not over, especially for the person who fled. Without a doubt, he will hit the same "upper limit of loving" in his next relationship, and the same choice will be before him, probably in an exaggerated form. (Wherever you go, there you are!) And for the person who was "left," there are many lessons still to be dealt with: What in you attracted someone who would leave? Do you harbor a fear of intimacy that matches or complements the one that drove your partner away? Are you ready to go deeper in relationship and create a bond that is less vulnerable to fear? For both you and your partner, the relationship will not be complete until you tell the next truth and find the next level of intimacy *within* yourselves. In such a scenario, both members would do better to hang in there, seek counseling, and do whatever it takes to come to terms with the fears that drove you apart *before* you attempt to leave or start a new relationship.

"Until death do you part" is a vow not to be taken lightly, for it is a very significant promise. A couple must make every effort to work through difficulties in their relationship and sincerely strive to join and go deeper with each other through times of hardship. At the same time, the marriage vow is not meant to be an albatross of eternal punishment. Two wrongs do not make a right, and if you made a decision in a stupor—or the decision you made is no longer life-enhancing—you only compound it if you stay where you do not belong.

The same loving God who created marriage also created the cycles of life. Nothing lives forever, except love and true relationship, which is ultimately spiritual. Bodies come and go, as do sex, romance, and particular forms of connections between human beings. To stay together in pain is a denial of your right to be happy, and to part in love is an affirmation of that same right. Give your relationship your whole heart, and if and when the time comes for your lives to change, do your very best to keep your heart open in the process. You may lose a temporary husband or wife, but gain a lifetime friend.

<hr/>

∾∾

Rashke and Russ:
I Loved Him Enough to Leave Him

Some lives are destined to be joined for a moment in time. When I saw Russ on the racquetball court 20 years ago, I knew I would marry him. I don't regret that choice. Russ loved me unconditionally in a way in which I had not been loved before, nor have been since. He has a kind and generous heart, and a compassion that flows through his work as a pediatrician as well as through his life.

When I married Russ, I was a bud choking in a field of weeds and confusion, uncertain of who I was and not sure of the path I needed to take. Under the wings of Russ's uncondi-

tional love, I was able to explore myself and what life was all about—and for this I will always be grateful to him. I often felt like a Thumbelina doll gently held in his strong hands, protected from life—and as much as I liked this feeling, I also resented it. I needed to explore, feel the pain, and find my own successes and failures in order to find out who I was—all by myself. As I searched and discovered this being inside of me, Russ and I remained dear friends and companions—but the marriage began to fade.

I loved Russ too much to keep him in a relationship that wasn't fulfilling for him, and in which he could not bloom to his full potential. My strength drained him, and his protectiveness smothered my soul. Yet I loved him with all my heart. I loved him enough to leave him.

Would he feel resentful or used? Yes, he would have, if he were not made of the strong, compassionate substance that permeated his very being. Instead, Russ understood that it was the right choice to go our separate ways. Russ is a man who accommodates, reveres, serves, and loves people. Every day he touches the lives of the children and parents who cross his path. He is gentle, easy, casual in his relating, yet passionate and intense about what he believes in. He felt that way about our marriage, he felt that way about me, and he feels that way about his life today. Russ loves life, and with this love, offers freedom to everyone he touches.

We were married 12 years and have been divorced for seven. We still keep in touch. Russ has remarried; in fact, I introduced him to his wife. But he will always be the love of my life.

Do I regret divorcing him? No. Do I regret marrying him? No. Not all marriages are meant to last a lifetime. While they last, however, they provide fertile soil for the growth of two people and two souls. That's what my marriage to Russ did for me.

I feel very lucky to have spent 12 years with Russ and very blessed to have him continue to be my friend. A few people in our lives leave an imprint on our soul, and that's what Russ has done for me.

c h a p t e r 4

Stop the Insanity

Turning Scars into Stars

"A wise man will make haste to forgive, because he knows the full value of time and will not suffer it to pass away in unnecessary pain."

— Rambler

If you send a rat down a maze where it finds a piece of cheese, the rodent will make its way through the maze again and again. If you take the cheese away, the rat will make a few more trips through the maze, but after it repeatedly fails to get a reward, the creature will give up and find no motivation to travel that route.

The difference between rats and humans is that we continue to travel down mazes that have no cheese at the end. Our minds are so powerful that we can convince ourselves that we are getting something valuable out of a situation in which we are actually losing. As a famous marriage counselor noted:

**If something you are doing is not working,
doing more of it will not work better.**

If you are truly intent on making a better life for yourself, stop struggling with your ex-partner. The blame game doesn't work—it never has and never will. When you set out on a course of fault-finding, both you and your partner lose. For every blame you lay on your partner, he or she will find one to lay on you, and both of you will keep binding yourselves in circles that become only tighter and more suffocating. *To belittle is to be little.*

To find fault is to lose sight of the real purpose of your relationship, which is to grow in love and become more magnificent. This noble purpose continues and may even expand after the end of your romantic, sexual, or marital connection. If, at the prompting of shaky love, you insist on making yourself or your partner wrong for the failure of your relationship, you will overlook and delay the joy that is available now. Big Love, on the other hand, recognizes that to receive what you want, you must shift your focus from what you do not want, to what your heart truly desires.

Insanity: Doing the same thing in the same way and expecting a different result.

A Course in Miracles[3] asks, "Do you prefer that you be right or happy?" You may have a long list of reasonable arguments to support your position that the breakup was your partner's fault. You may have many friends who agree with you. You may even have a wealth of evidence that would stand up (or has) in a court of law, pointing to your partner's culpability and indebtedness. But if your heart is embroiled in bitterness, anger, self-pity, righteousness, or a sense of victimization, you are hurting yourself more than you can afford. As you sit by the door of the prison of judgment to which you have confined your partner, you must stay in jail with him. Give your partner his freedom, and gain your own.

You lose equally, or more so, if you burden yourself with guilt. Beating yourself up for the breakup, or regretting errors that you made in the relationship, is just as self-defeating as condemning your partner. The question is not, "Whose fault was it?" It is, "What can we do now to create the kind of relationship we will enjoy?"

A Zen story tells of two monks who were walking through a forest when they encountered a woman standing on the bank of a stream she was unable to ford. After assessing the lady's dilemma, one monk picked her up in his arms, carried her across the stream, and placed her gently on the far bank. The other monk watched aghast, for the rules of their order forbade touching women. The two ascetics walked on, but the second monk fumed for a long time. Finally he blurted out, "You know that touching a woman is against our principles!" With that, the other monk turned to him and calmly answered, "I put her down an hour ago. You, however, are still carrying her."

When we carry past hurts and grievances into the present moment, we cloud our vision and miss the love and beauty before us. Dr. Gerald Jampolsky, author of the popular book *Love is Letting Go of Fear*, [4] defines forgiveness as "giving up all hope for a better past."

Your happiness depends not on what happened in the past, but what you do with the moment at hand.

Letting Go, Moving On

Take a piece of paper and write down every judgment you have held about your former partner. Record everything he or she has ever done that has hurt you, and every emotion those actions generated within you. List the losses you believe that he or she has caused you. Be extremely thorough to include every negative thing you can think of about your partner and your relationship.

When you feel complete, take the paper and conduct a burning bowl ceremony. Place the paper in a bowl and set it aflame with this or a similar statement:

"[Full name of your ex-partner], I hereby release you and myself from our past. I let go of the pain I have felt with you, and any other negative emotions that no longer serve me. I let go of the fears and judgments that have kept you and me small. I let you be exactly who you are, and I forever give up trying to change you. I honor who you are, and I appreciate the gifts and blessings you and our relationship have brought into my life. I acknowledge both of us for doing the best we could. Now I allow you to live your life, and I allow myself to live mine. I free you and myself to take our next steps to greater good. I bless and liberate both of us, that we may each fulfill our hearts' desires and life purpose."

Conduct the ceremony in a safe, private place, alone or with one or two supportive friends. (If you are on good terms with your partner, you might do it together.) Give yourself plenty of time to feel and be with the process. Meditate, contemplate, or pray before the act to attune yourself to the purpose. If you conduct this ceremony with a sincere intention, you will feel extraordinarily free and alive, move your relationship with your ex into a new dimension, and eliminate needless pain and heartache.

A BETTER WAY

Many of us have spent a great deal of time analyzing and rehashing the issues of our relationships. Some of us have processed our relationships so intensely that we lose sight of the love, joy, and appreciation we felt when the relationship began.

Eventually we grow weary of dissecting our experiences, relationships, and selves. At some point we declare, silently or audibly, *"There must be a better way."* At that moment we become teachable. As long as we believe that we are right and the way we have been seeing the situation is the only way, our chances of finding peace are minimal. Consider that your partner's experience is just as valid for her or him as your experience is for you. Truth in relationships is not an either/or matter. Each of you looks upon any situation from your own perspective. Both of your viewpoints are valid, yet incomplete.

Arguing does not work; *love works*.

One moment of offering unconditional love can short-circuit and avoid many hours of fruitless emotional wrestling.

When you find greater value in harmony than in discord, the fighting will stop, and your relationship will be a source of dear reward. If you find yourself arguing, do your best to return to peace as quickly as you can. The best way to defuse an argument is to remember that *anyone can argue with your opinions, but no one can argue with your experience.* Both you and your partner have every right to feel what you are feeling, without having to decide whose feelings are more correct. Feelings are neither right nor wrong; they just are. The mind wants to think, the emotions want to experience, and the heart wants to heal.

You will come to resolution when you take joy in your partner's happiness rather than reinforcing his inadequacy or pain. In that moment, you will open the door to your own success, as well. As *A Course in Miracles* poetically declares, "It will be given you to see your brother's worth when all you want for him is peace. And what you want for him you will receive." All healing occurs on common ground.

Post-Breakup Scenarios

1. Ongoing warfare: The couple's interaction centers around blame, attack, defensiveness, and open hostility. Partners hurl cruel and unkind barbs at each other and speak disparagingly of each other to friends, who are recruited as allies to take sides. One or both partners consider themselves a victim and seek retribution. Money, property, and children become political footballs in each partner's fruitless struggle to be right.

2. Silent warfare: Partners do not speak to each other, and may move out of the sphere of each other's lives, but inwardly bear pain, anger, guilt, or resentment. Thinking or speaking about the other partner leads to upset and criticism of self or others.

3. Debilitating ambiguity: Partners, not having come to a sense of completion or resolution about their relationship, continue to indulge aspects of their romance through word, innuendo, or sexuality. One or both partners fantasize or talk about getting back together, yet no overt steps are taken in that direction. An on-again, off-again relationship ensues, neither partner gets on with his or her life, and the relationship is more debilitating than empowering.

4. One-sided warfare: One partner has released the relationship, but the other still clings. He or she continues to carry a sense of victimization, or fruitlessly hopes to reconcile. One partner moves on with his or her life, while the other partner remains stuck in pain or fantasy.

5. Peaceful silence: Both partners feel complete with the relationship, and get on with their lives. They have little or no interaction, and they are emotionally free of their history together.

6. Appreciative memory: Partners have little or no interaction but think fondly or kindly of their each other and the relationship and appreciate its role in their growth.

7. Friendly interaction: Partners see each other socially or in the course of child care, and cooperate in a positive and amiable manner.

8. Supportive interaction: Partners go beyond their legal obligations or social expectations, speak kindly of each other, and make an effort to brighten each other's lives.

9. Greater love: Partners meet at a deeper and more rewarding level of love; celebrate their past and current relationship as a gift and blessing; and demonstrate gratefulness to each other for their contributions to each other's growth, healing, and aliveness.

If you are to have a different (and better) relationship, you are going to have to approach it from a different angle. You do not need to work harder; you need to work smarter. Peace, release, compassion, and supportive thoughts, words, and actions always work smarter than separateness, resentment, and backbiting. If you and your partner are not compatible, there is no law that says you must live, sleep, or spend a lot of time together. But neither is there a law that says you must throw each other out of your hearts. You have every right to stay mad or distant for the rest of your life, but you also have the right to wake up from the nightmare and choose peace. Peace is the most practical attitude in the world, for it gets results more fundamentally and for a longer term than conflict, the "rewards" of which are empty. You may get the house, but if you lose a friend forever, you have made a lousy deal. Give yourself the gift of releasing your partner, your past, and yourself now, so that you may get on with the very important business of building a future entirely more wonderful.

"Life is short and we have never too much time for gladdening the hearts of those who are traveling the dark journey with us. Oh be swift to love, make haste to be kind."
— Henri Frederick Amiel

⍟⍟
Sherri and Jeff:
We Learned How to Forgive and Forget

When I married Jeff, I loved him more than life itself. I couldn't imagine living without him; given the circumstances, I would have gladly given my life to save his. We lived together nine years and had a daughter, Kira, who was three when Jeff fell in love with my best friend and sister-in-law, Mandy, and left me to marry her.

My hurt was beyond words. I spoke to Jeff as seldom as possible and avoided seeing him. Whatever contact we had usually ended in a battle. I simply wrote Mandy off with the vow that I would never look at her face again as long as I lived. Jeff had run us into the ground financially with their affair, and when he moved out of state to be with Mandy, collecting child support was virtually impossible, which only added to my hostility. Kira quickly became a pawn in our war. As long as Jeff wasn't paying support, I refused to let him see our daughter, under the firm conviction that if he wanted to be a father, he had to share in the financial responsibility and not just pop in and out of her life whenever it suited him.

Three years after our breakup, Jeff wrote me a three-page letter of apology asking for my forgiveness. I filed it away, refusing to believe it was anything but an attempt to con me, as he had done so many times in the past. It took seven more years for my anger to dissipate enough for me to carry on a decent conversation with him or spend any amount of time in his presence. Mandy was another matter; I still would not allow her within my sight. If Jeff wanted to see Kira, he and I would have to make the exchange in town, and if Mandy was with him, she would have to stay out of sight.

Ten years had passed when something unexpected happened.

My mother, who had also been deeply hurt by Jeff's betrayal, reconsidered her hostility and wrote Jeff and Mandy a letter asking for their forgiveness. I was shocked when she told me. They wrote my mother a letter in response, filled with appreciation for her sentiments. They told her that they stood in their kitchen and cried as they read her letter together. When I heard those words, I felt a slight softening in my own heart toward them, but not enough to change anything on the outside. I still didn't trust either of them as far as I could throw them.

Kira became the victim of all our upset, and her teenage rebellion reflected that position. By age 13 she had been caught shoplifting twice, and life with her was one constant battle of wills. Then, during the summer she turned 18, while Kira was staying at our vacation home in Minnesota, she was arrested for theft. Jeff was the first to find out, and that weekend he and I spent more time talking on the phone than we had in all the previous 15 years. I rushed to Minnesota while Jeff and I continued to communicate; it was the first time we had worked together on anything since the breakup of our marriage.

Jeff flew up to see Kira and invited me to come and meet him for dinner. I still didn't trust him or myself enough to be alone with him, so I picked a spot to meet that was safe—the local Dairy Queen. As we sat together talking for the first time in so many years, much of our conversation was spent sharing news about old mutual friends. Suddenly I realized our conversation was no different from that of two old friends catching up, and I began to relax my guard. When Jeff told me that he, too, had been studying and practicing A Course in Miracles, *I dropped my wall of protection, let go of my distrust, and opened my heart.*

We talked well into the night, until Kira walked into the house at 1 A.M. to find us sitting together talking and laughing. The expression on her face was something we will never forget—it was a look of pure disbelief! Jeff and I felt the same way; neither of us could believe what was happening. We spent the next three days together dealing with Kira's legal mess—talking to the lawyer, D.A., and the psychologist. Jeff slept in my van behind the house, spent time with us on the lake, and shared meals and family time together. We all remained in a state of shock.

Kira was put on probation, and we both decided it would be best if she lived with Jeff. But the miracle was only half completed— I still had Mandy to deal with. I had kept my vow, and we'd had virtually no communication. The few times I called to talk to Jeff or Kira, if Mandy answered the phone, I would simply ask for one of them without acknowledging her in any way.

The opportunity to break my vow came when I had to call Jeff regarding Kira's legal situation. Mandy answered the phone and told me that Jeff was out of town. I hesitated, then figured, "Now is the time," and proceeded to share with Mandy what I had planned to tell Jeff. We talked for nearly 20 minutes. Three months later, I broke the rest of my vow. On my way to visit my folks in Florida, I stopped in Tallahassee to see Kira. When I got there, no one was home, so I took a seat in the living room. An hour later, Mandy arrived home from work. I answered the door, greeting her, "Welcome home." Then we sat down and spent the evening catching up while we waited for Jeff to come home. It was as if we were picking up from where we left off as best friends, merely forgetting that 15 years had gone by since then, as well as what had happened during those years. Everything else was the same. When Jeff got home, he joined us, and we continued. I ended up sleeping in the guest room that night as well as the next, while we spent time together healing our relationships.

Seven years have passed since our miracle. We are all family once again, and best friends. We visit each other, stay in touch, share our lives and families, and love as if I had never been hurt. It's a gift we treasure deeply, and we will all be eternally grateful that we learned how to forgive and forget.

c h a p t e r 5

From Breakup to Breakthrough

Making Divorce Work on your Behalf

"What the caterpillar calls the end of the world, the master calls a butterfly."

— Richard Bach[5]

A divorce or breakup is not the worst thing that can happen to you; but living in fear, pain, or frustration *is* the worst thing that can happen. Be careful not to write your breakup off as a tragedy. Seen from a higher perspective, it could be the best thing that ever happened to you. You may have lost a partner but regained your soul. With your soul intact, you are empowered to recreate your relationship from a point of strength, not weakness.

Take Martin and Evie, for example. They were a highly respected couple in my community who had established a thriving business. Their marriage was regarded as a model of love and integrity. Then, after ten years of being together, the roles they had fallen into began to strangle them, and being together became a struggle. Evie and Martin put up a strong front for a while, and then, after significant soul-searching, announced that they were getting divorced. Instantly, shock waves rippled through the community. "If Martin and Evie could break up, is *any* marriage secure?" onlookers murmured fearfully.

Then, in the wake of their breakup, we all beheld a miracle. Both Martin and Evie began to thrive in ways they had not experienced in their marriage. Martin, who had been reclusive, brainy, and physically unhealthy, gained color in his cheeks, began to dress fashionably, and literally came to life. He dated energetic women and frequented local dance clubs. The former bookworm took piano lessons and actually became quite a good musician. Everything about Martin took on a new glow and vitality.

Evie, too, stepped into her own power. While she had allowed Martin to make most of the decisions in their marriage, she took charge of her own life, traveled, and established her own business. Whereas most people had seen Evie as half of an entity, now she developed her own identity and created a rewarding relationship with a man entirely unlike her former husband. Both Martin and Evie blossomed in their own right and served as an important example to a community that had looked on their divorce with anxiety and disdain.

***Sometimes what looks like a disaster is
a miracle in the making.***

The purpose of relationship is to empower both partners to discover and express their highest potential. When a marriage implodes and inhibits the expression of that potential, it is no longer serving its function. In many cases, passion may be rekindled through deeper communication, counseling, and inner transformational work by one or both partners; this is certainly the optimal path. But if it cannot, the couple must revisit their contract and do whatever it takes to renew their life force. *Your first and foremost responsibility is to be fully alive.* Then you really have something to offer to your relationship, friends, and the world.

A Course in Miracles advises us, "You do not know what anything is for," and "some of your greatest advances you have judged as failures, and some of your deepest retreats you have evaluated as success." From the human perspective, it is extremely difficult to know how any one event fits into the Big Picture. From the divine perspective, all is well, and every experience ultimately contributes to our awakening.

Consider this account illustrating the power of perspective: In the early 1900s, a shoe manufacturer sent a salesman to Africa to expand their market. After a few weeks in the foreign land, the rep sent a telegram to the home office: *"Disaster! Disaster! These people do not wear shoes. Cancel production immediately."*

Later that year, a salesman from another shoe manufacturer traveled to the same country, also in hopes of growing the company's client base. Soon their headquarters, too, received a telegram. This one read: *"Opportunity! Opportunity! These people do not wear shoes. Triple production immediately."*

Everything you experience depends on the vision you use.

I learned about perspective from my friends Bill and Patricia, whom I love to visit at their Pennsylvania country home. Bill is a spry octogenarian with rich wisdom fueled by a delightfully youthful attitude. One evening while the three of us were relaxing in their living room, I decided to go into the kitchen to make some tea. Not seeing a readily available teakettle, I grabbed a Pyrex coffeepot from the Mr. Coffee machine, filled it with water, and put it on the gas stovetop to boil.

A few minutes later, we smelled something burning in the kitchen and ran to see what it was. To my great embarrassment, I discovered that I had left the pot's plastic handle too close to the flame, and it was ablaze! Quickly I blew the fire out, and after a moment of adrenaline flow, we breathed a sigh of relief.

Sheepishly I turned to my hosts and apologized for ruining the handle on their Pyrex pot. Then, feeling guilty, I waited for a rebuke. Instead, Bill smiled and exclaimed, "My goodness, Alan, I had no idea you were such a good fireman!"

Immediately, I felt a sense of lightness and relief. Bill's words and attitude instantly transformed a clumsy moment into one of joy and laughter. Bill taught me that . . .

Guilt, punishment, and sorrow are not absolutes that the universe doles out to us; they are attitudinal choices we make, which we can transform at any moment.

Pain happens, but suffering is optional. It is impossible to walk through life without experiencing pain. But how long we milk it or wallow in it is up to us. Consider the cat who sleeps beneath a car when she hears the driver turn on the engine. Instantly the cat darts from the auto, and within a few seconds finds another resting place several yards away. Within a few moments, the feline is as relaxed as she was before she had to move. The cat does not give the driver the finger, call all her friends to recount the incident endlessly, or go on a TV talk show to rant about the injustices inflicted upon sleeping cats. Instinctively, the cat realizes that all of these actions would just waste her time and energy, which could be put to much better use by simply finding another place to rest and going right ahead with her relaxing routine.

We can use relationship breakups to justify self-pity or righteous indignation, or we can use them as a stepping stone to a richer quality of living. In this world of illusions, we are often tempted to judge by appearances, but in the long run, many things are unfolding that are not obvious from within the drama. In sports, the history books never record a game's score at halftime; that's forgotten once the final score is tallied. As you align your vision with Big Love, the gifts in your life become your reality, and the problems that led you to the gifts disappear into dust. *A Course in Miracles* reminds us: "All your past except its beauty is gone, and nothing is left but a blessing."

Everything serves.

If you want to skyrocket ahead in your personal growth, ask this question of every experience: *How does this event contribute to greater good in my life?* If you can get into the spirit of the inquiry and allow the voice of trust to speak louder than that of insecurity, you will open the door to miracles in your relationships (and all aspects of your life) and never again doubt that we live in a benevolent universe.

During a visit to Dallas, my friend Lisa and I were taking a walk around a lake in a park, where I was disturbed to see a ring of debris encircling the lake. This long, unsightly strip was filled with plastic bottles, aluminum cans, and splintered pieces of wood. When I asked Lisa if the lake shore was always so grimy, she explained that a heavy storm had recently churned the waters and sent all kinds of junk from the depths of the lake to the shore. Later, a cleaning crew would walk along the path and methodically scoop up the garbage.

Then I understood: The storm was a blessing. The high winds and tumultuous waves elicited a huge volume of unseen trash, which the tide brought to one place where it could be cleaned up easily.

A relationship ending may dredge up all sorts of gnarly thoughts, feelings, and actions that are not pretty and which may be downright embarrassing to admit; indeed, such an experience can bring forth the worst in us. But, used correctly, it can bring forth the best in us. Yes, garbage comes to the surface, but if it is dealt with in the light, the waters are purified in a way they never could have been if the winds had remained placid. In the long run, your experience may have saved you time, energy, and pain that you do not comprehend, and opened you to a new depth of strength, honesty, appreciation, and communication. If you can see—even for a moment—through the eyes of Big Love, you will find peace that shaky love could never bestow.

If the dissolution of your relationship peeled you away from illusions, shattered limits you thought were real, or motivated you to tap into inner power that you did not even know you had, then I say, "Bravo!" And if your divorce settlement cost you money that you begrudge, consider that millions of people pay thousands of dollars for personal growth seminars and consciousness trainings. Some one-week courses cost as much as $5,000, followed by the follow-up, and then the follow-up to the follow-up. If you made a huge leap of growth as a result of your divorce, you may have gotten a bargain—for a smaller price than it would have cost you to attend a posh seminar.

And if all else fails, just laugh it off. Psychologists tell us that one of the signs of psychosis is an absence of a sense of humor; if you can't laugh at something, you haven't seen the whole truth about it. To be able to make fun of a situation, no matter how serious it would seem to be, is a sure sign of mastery and spiritual advancement.

The only important question to ask in the aftermath of a separation is, "How am I different?" How have you grown, how has your life changed, and who are you now that is greater than who you were? If you can answer these questions with honest appreciation, you will become a true alchemist, transmuting lead into gold, and you will find immeasurable value in your relationship—including your breakup—for the rest of your life.

ॐ ॐ

Sara and Steven:
Today I Am Different

"I know it's not going to be easy, but I want you to be my wife. . . . Will you marry me?" What a strange way for Steven to propose to me—yet I didn't think of that at the time. I just heard those four magic words, that awesome question that I had obsessed over ever since I was a little girl. Visions of lace and vows, romance and rings danced in my mind. There had been problems in our relationship, control issues, flirtations, and yet I loved this

man. "Nothing is perfect," I tried to assure myself. Besides, we were standing in front of the Western Wall in Jerusalem, the holiest place in Judaism. Surely God would bless this union.

We returned to the States amidst a maze of parties and preparations. This would be the wedding reception of the decade, and soon after, we would break ground on our magnificent new home. From all outward appearances, we were living the American Dream on eight pristine acres of farm land in the countryside of Georgia.

Our wedding was a blur of excess, followed by a Hawaiian honeymoon shared with two other couples. Bizarre as that was, it seemed a wise decision, since my new spouse was more relaxed in the presence of these friends who concurred that premarital jitters were understandable for a wealthy 45-year-old bachelor.

By this point, Steven's temper tantrums had escalated to a frightening crescendo, which left my stomach in perpetual spasm. Although on some level I was scared and apprehensive, in many ways this off-balanced feeling felt strangely familiar. I had been raised by a European mother who dished out heavy doses of criticism, anger, and guilt. I was home again. For better or worse, I committed to God, my husband, and myself to make it work.

Building our dream home turned into a nightmare—everything that could possibly go askew did so, to its extreme. Thousands of dollars of marble imported from Italy arrived in the wrong color—six times! A circular staircase had to be redesigned, holding up the progress of the second floor for eight months. The swimming pool was so misaligned that the contractor agreed to start over. As the one-year project went into its third year, my health severely deteriorated. The stresses of trying to make this experience tolerable became overwhelming. If Steven had something to be displeased about before, these new circumstances fueled his unrelenting wrath. The aftermath of no-show workmen, delivery holdups, and escalating costs were dropped on me like bombs each night as I became a scapegoat for my husband's frustrations. Eventually, nothing I did was acceptable. No telephone conversation, no dress I wore, no decision I made pleased my self-appointed surrogate parent. By the time we moved into this looming albatross, I was physically and emotionally depleted. To ensure that our pastel-colored castle was protected, a chemical cloud of Scotch Guard was sprayed over every inch of its 7,000 square feet. My health got worse, much worse. Throbbing headaches accompanied nausea. Persistent sore throats gave way to high fever and muscle pains; unrelenting exhaustion filled my waking hours, while terror reigned over sleepless nights.

Doctors offered little help or explanation. "It's all in your head," many said. Others said little, but thought and acted that way. Steven grew more and more impatient with my frailty. We had lots of social obligations to fulfill. Not wanting to displease him, I regularly put on a smile and forced myself to be gracious at a midnight fund-raiser or political dinner meant to enhance his career. Three years of devastating illness culminated in what was finally diagnosed as chemical sensitivity and Chronic Fatigue Syndrome (CFS). My attempt to create something beautiful had turned into a bad dream, taking my health with it.

While I was in a California clinic trying to strengthen my immune system, Steven showed up and asked for a divorce. I remember sitting on the edge of my bed, heartbroken, tears cascading, while I cradled my fragile body.

"You've been a good wife," he assured me. "This is not your fault. I should never have gotten married. You gave me 110 percent, much more than I gave you. At least you won't have to worry about money. That won't be a problem. You'll get yourself well and get on with your life," he tried to comfort me.

I stayed in the clinic crying for another six weeks, putting myself through more exhaustive measures in an effort to heal. This new reality was terrifying. What would I do? I still loved him deeply. How could I take care of myself when I was bedridden most of the time? The words "in sickness and in health" taunted me as I tried to envision an uncertain future.

My return to Georgia was met with a very different attitude from my soon-to-be-ex. "You better get yourself a good lawyer," he told me. "I don't see any need for you to continue to live in our summer house. An apartment should suffice." I soon uncovered the reason for his callous new posture—her name was Shelly, and they had been involved for over a year. The terror of a debilitating illness now teamed up with betrayal and financial uncertainty. I was too weak to enter into a legal battle with this influential man. Yet, the uncertainty of CFS coupled with my shaky professional status forced me to confront a ruthless situation. The stresses of lawyers and Steven's monstrous behavior depleted my health even more. At one point, some friends of his came forth and told the truth about the many shams involving my spouse. "There's a right and wrong in life," they stated, "and this treatment of you is wrong, very wrong." Their words helped pull me through those long months of legal atrocities. It looked like I would lose my home and adequate support for an illness that had no end in sight.

Then, by an act of faith and God's masterful presence, a succession of miracles occurred, providing the money necessary for me to continue. A year after we separated, I attended a Course in Miracles *conference in Virginia. I had righteously held on to my well-deserved anger, often reviewing the heinous acts of my former husband—all of which depleted me even more. There was little I could eat or wear or be in close proximity to; my environmental sensitivities had compounded, creating a very limited existence for me. Yet, there I was listening to the words of the keynote speaker: "Your life will truly start working when you see everything in it as a miracle: the divorce, the illness, the loss in whatever form it takes. Forgiveness is the key. . . ."*

I sat there, astonished. Those words reached down and tugged at my soul. Their resonance stirred me, waking me from a long hibernation of closed mind and heart. Tears welled up in my eyes. I rose from the chair and somehow made my way out of the building to an adjacent wooded area. Thoughts swirled within me, forcing through like young blades of grass in fertile soil. I felt heady, alive for the first time in years. Here I was surrounded by friends in an entirely new life that I believed would one day hold great promise. "But what about the illness?" my ego chided. It's true, the illness had been devastating. Yet, it was also responsible for bringing me into spiritual awareness, for exposing me to much good and truth. I had learned to view life in a very precious way.

"But what about the heart-wrenching infidelities and Shelly?" my ego retaliated. I knelt down on a blanket of autumn leaves beneath the trees. Rays of sunshine cascaded through the elms as I looked toward heaven for an answer. . . . Would I really want to be married to Steven today? His intense lifestyle seemed so foreign to mine, which was now characterized by peace and simplicity. It may have taken a horrible illness and a humiliating divorce for me to realize that, yet its truth was evident. If not for Shelly, we might still be married—two mismatched people, with only one committed to making it work. "Bless him," whispered the fragrant breezes. "Bless it all."

In that moment, I knew what I had to do. There was a telephone in sight, and I headed for it. Moments later I was put through to Steven's office. When I shared my realizations with him, his surprise was evident. I pushed on, "I want you to know that I wish you well and will always keep you in my prayers." A heavy breath of tears choked through the wire as he responded. "I love you, and I'm sorry for all that has happened." And then as if by magic, an expansive wave of forgiveness washed over me, releasing me from the muck I had mired in for far too long. My heart expanded, overflowing with a merciful warmth and knowingness that somehow I'd be well again.

Seven years have passed since that September morning. There have been some setbacks and many dragons to be slain. Yet today, I am different. My life is gentler, sweeter in many ways. Adversity has been a good teacher. My robust health is returning. Those long years of illness provided an invaluable education in holistic med-

icine. And I ultimately received a divorce settlement that included the summer house I loved.

There has been an emotional healing as well; I now hold a new paradigm for relationships. My license plate serves as a constant reminder: BELIEVE. I am in touch with my needs and with my soul. When I look back at the awesome changes I have experienced, I remember that profound day when my healing began. Its truth for me has been proven many times over: Through forgiveness, all things are possible.

c h a p t e r   6

Beyond the Pain

Stepping into Strength

*"Many of us spend our whole lives running from feeling with the
mistaken belief that you cannot bear the pain. But you have
already borne the pain. What you have not done is feel
all you are beyond that pain."*

— Kahlil Gibran

The story is told about a family who was expecting the
father's boss and his wife for dinner. A few minutes before
the guests were to arrive, one of the children noticed a huge
dead rhinoceros's head lying on the center of the dining room
table, oozing blood onto the table. Quickly the family called a
meeting to try to figure out how to deal with the unsightly mess.
After some discussion they decided to simply leave the rhinoceros head there and hope no one would notice.

While this remedy seems ridiculous, it is not much more exaggerated than the ways that some of us have dealt with our pain.
When we ignore or distract ourselves from an unpleasant situation, we miss the gift; the mess is trying to get our attention so that
we may grow through healing it. All addictive behaviors are
unconsciously fueled by denial, as the addict numbs himself in a

pastime that provides temporary relief, but only drives the original pain and problem deeper. The only cure for pain is to look upon it honestly and acknowledge the message it has come to bring you.

In the wake of a relationship or marriage breakup, we may be tempted to go into denial about the discomfort we feel. Here are the most common forms of denial:

1. **Overt denial:** Making believe that you don't care; smiling, cracking jokes; acting as if nothing has happened; passing off the breakup with glib metaphors such as "There are other fish in the sea."

2. **Blaming:** Criticizing the former partner for the failure of the relationship; fault-finding; making statements such as "He was such a jerk; I can't believe I ever liked him."

3. **Guilt:** Punishing yourself for mistakes or for the failure of the relationship—"If only I'd been a better person or had done more."

4. **Rebounding:** Quickly jumping into another relationship to mask the pain lingering from the last one.

5. **Falling back on addiction:** Using a favored addiction to numb the pain.

Common Ways We Numb or Distract Ourselves from Emotional Pain

Drinking	Taking drugs	Overeating
Workaholism	Incessant busyness	Compulsive sex
Oversleeping	Watching television	Computer/Internet
Going to movies	Making money	Amassing worldly power

Gambling	Self-help seminars	Reading romance novels
Obsessive exercise	Cleaning	Talking on the telephone
Paperwork	Home improvement	Fantasy lover

Many of the above activities are innocent, potentially enjoyable, and may indeed provide healthy relief during a time of stress. If you engage in them continually and addictively, however, you are running away from facing a truth of some sort. When confronted with the temptation to slip into your addiction of choice, you have a golden opportunity to reprogram a pattern that has probably kept you feeling and acting small for a long time.

THE WAY OUT

Notice, as your hand reaches for the refrigerator handle or TV remote control, whether you are really hungry or desire to watch a particular program; or if you are grasping for a distraction. If you find yourself running on automatic, stop, collect yourself for a moment, take a deep breath, and ask yourself, "What is my predominant feeling right now?" Most likely you will notice that you are feeling lonely, angry, frustrated, or confused. Such uncomfortable feelings are not to be run from, but are to be embraced as invitations to deeper self-awareness, acceptance, and constructive action. Each feeling that you courageously face and rechannel will lift you to higher ground from which you will see how to avoid trudging through the same hell next time. Here are some common feelings you may be tempted to run from, and the positive messages they may be offering you:

Feeling:	Message:
Sadness	*Get in touch with your heart's desire*
Loneliness	*Reach out and make contact*
Fear	*Recognize that you are not limited*
Anger	*Uncover self-criticism; reclaim responsibility*
Resentment	*Honor self-worth*
Guilt	*Recognize innocence; embrace all parts of self*
Powerlessness	*Discover the power within*
Mistrust	*Place trust in the process rather than the person*
Sexual need	*Establish true intimacy*
Being stuck	*Stimulate action over analysis*

Here is a technique to discover the message a negative feeling seeks to deliver to you:

Close your eyes, take a deep breath, and imagine sitting in a quiet, peaceful place. In your mind's eye, take your predominant feeling and place it on a table in front of you. Give the feeling a name, size, shape, color, dimension, texture, and voice. Imagine that the feeling, no matter how ugly it appears, is your friend, and it has come to give you a message. Then ask it, "[*name of feeling*], what is the message or the gift you have come to give me?" Then wait quietly and listen within you. When you feel ready, take a pen to paper and record everything the feeling wants you to know.

You will be amazed and delighted to discover that what you thought was your bitter enemy turns out to be a precious friend. If you tell the truth about your feelings without denying them, you are on the road to eliminating the source of your painful emotions, rather than being tossed about by the waves they have set in motion.

DENIAL BUSTERS

"Okay, I'm ready and willing to be bigger than denial," you affirm. "How, then, can I master it?"

The best way to sidestep denial is to take positive, direct, healthy steps to deal with your hurtful feelings in the wake of a broken relationship:

1. Enter into constructive counseling or therapy: Find a good professional counselor or therapist who can give you quality attention and help you sort out your feelings, learn from your experience, and move on to a more rewarding relationship.

Taking the step to get counseling does not mean that there's anything wrong with you; to the contrary, it is an affirmation of self-love and nurturing. You are valuing yourself enough to find ways to discover and express your true beauty, power, and greatness.

When choosing a counselor, be sure that she or he is a qualified individual you can trust. Your theropeutic relationship will be emotionally intimate, and you must feel safe to open up and express yourself. Be careful to avoid therapists who label you or try to fit you into the party line of their belief system or religion. You need to find more worth in who *you* are—not become someone else's idea of how you should be.

Make your counseling goal to move through your process in a short time. In most cases, three to six months should be sufficient to gain insight and work through your current situation. If you find real value in your counseling relationship and wish to go on to explore other, deeper aspects of your life, then you may choose to do so.

2. Talk to a supportive friend: Sometimes a good friend can offer you valuable listening and caring. Expressing your thoughts and feelings without a critical response can be quite liberating. If you feel safe with friends who will listen to you without judgment, ask them for some time. A true friend will be happy to be there for you in your time of need.

3. Join a support group: Get involved with an organization you can attend regularly, and enjoy fellowship with people on a parallel path. Such an association can make all the difference between the frustration of trying to work through a difficult time by yourself, and the empowerment of a network of peers who can uphold you as you build your strength. Below are some organizations with a positive spiritual orientation (addresses are listed in the endnotes section at the back of the book).

- *Course in Miracles* study groups[6]
- Unity churches[7]
- Religious Science churches[8]
- Self-Realization Fellowship[9]
- Association for Research and Enlightenment[10]
- Dale Carnegie courses[11]
- Yoga, tai chi, meditation classes (available at many adult schools and health centers)
- 12-step support groups (Sex & Love Addicts Anonymous, etc.)[12]

This list is by no means exhaustive; there are many worthy organizations and support groups. Be careful, however, not to get involved with groups that reinforce misery. Some organizations are stuck in the "victim" mode and encourage participants to stay trapped by endlessly repeating their dramas and commiserating over pain. While sharing your feelings is important and necessary, it is more important to gain tools to grow beyond your pain and get back on a creative track. You may evaluate your support group by the amount of strength, positivity, and growth you experience. If you feel more alive and empowered by attending, it is for you. If you walk away feeling drained, smaller, or angry at your parents or the opposite sex, it is not serving you.

4. Write in a journal: Regularly write down all of your thoughts and feelings about what is happening in you and around you. Do not censor or edit; whatever you are feeling is valid. Get *everything* onto paper. Do not show this journal to anyone; it is for your private use. You may ultimately choose to burn the notebook (or keep it), and it will have served an important purpose. (For an excellent practice, read *The Artist's Way*[14] by Julia Cameron.)

5. Enter into service: When you help someone in need, you discover that you're bigger than your problems. Volunteer at a nursing home, homeless shelter, big brother/big sister program, humane society, or any worthy organization. As you give love, you will be lifted and rewarded, and your problems will seem smaller. You will also be inspired by the people you help. As you give from your heart, you will understand the deeper meaning of relationship, and your romantic issues will take on a different perspective.

6. Pray and meditate: Create a regular connection with the Higher Power within you. Daily renew your soul through meaningful inspirational time. Beyond formal prayer or meditation, you might walk in the woods, listen to music, dance, paint, read, or enjoy any activity that elevates you to greater aliveness. Take a weekend retreat to be with yourself or participate in a seminar with others seeking to step back from their activities to establish their footing on sacred ground.

7. Have fun: Get out and do something new, different, playful, and outrageous. Don't just sit around feeling sorry for yourself, analyzing what went wrong. Listen for the voice of joy within you, and then follow its lead. You were not born to be miserable—you were born to love.

When your pain is great and you are most tempted to run away, you stand the greatest opportunity for real soul growth by standing firm, looking your feelings squarely in the eye, and asking, "What is the real truth about this?"

Honesty heals.

When you love *all* of you—not just the parts that you have been taught are socially acceptable—and tell the truth about what empowers you and what depletes you, you will be well on your way to the freedom you desire.

Your partner was and still is your friend. Sometimes the best learning partners are the ones who challenge us the most, drawing forth soul qualities from within us that we never would have developed if we had not been confronted. You do not need to seek or put up with abuse, but in retrospect you can see how an adversarial situation forced you to develop inner strength. *A Course in Miracles* teaches, "It is impossible to overestimate your brother's value" and "The only worthy response to your brother is appreciation."

And while you're at it, don't forget to send some appreciation your own way, too. You have been extremely courageous to come to Earth and grow through contrast. This has not been an easy place for most people, but it can be more comfortable if you let it be. The first step is truth, and the final step is love. In the end, they are the same.

ℰℰ

Vicki and Chad:
When I Care for Myself, Miracles Happen

When I married Chad at the age of 21, what I knew about engaging in productive relationships would have filled a matchbook cover. I had never seen my parents argue or work out problems. I also rarely saw them treat each other with kindness or tenderness. Their relationship was more traditional—me husband, you wife. Everyone just did their job, and real talk happened apart from the kids. They eventually separated, divorced, and reconnected.

So here I was in a relationship with a "nice young man" from a Father Knows Best*–type family. Their interaction was rosy on the surface, very role-bound and cordial, but not real. It was the '70s, and Chad smoked marijuana daily—harmless, we thought. If he knew how to build an effective marital relationship, the dope erased his memory. We were clueless young people who cared for each other but lacked information and skills.*

For reasons I won't go into now, I felt ashamed and undeserving of this "nice young man." I ran the household, managed the bills, and held down a full-time job. We talked more like a brother and sister than lovers. We had sex but no intimacy. We didn't know how.

I felt trapped and smothered, like I was dying. Chad kept asking me if I was happy, and I'd say yes—I didn't know how to say no. I described my situation to my gynecologist, who recommended a couple who worked as a marriage counseling team. I felt comfortable approaching my well-educated husband with the news, but to my shock, Chad harshly refused to enter into counseling, saying that not only was he not going, but neither was I.

I was miserable and felt stuck. I tried to tell myself that by now I should be happy, with two Saabs in the driveway, two beautiful children, and a nice townhouse in suburbia. I was also a workaholic, attending happy hours, doing shots, and, over time, engaging in two affairs.

By now, Chad and I had been married for nearly ten years. I secretly went to see a psychotherapist and told him that I was crazy. He said, "You're not crazy—you just need someone to talk to." We worked for six months before he decided it was time to call in my husband. I warned him that Chad would say, "Nothing's wrong, I forgive her, everything's okay," which is exactly what he said. The counselor told me, "Now you must decide what you'll do next."

I suggested to Chad that we take a honeymoon weekend in a raunchy hotel with a mirrored ceiling, and watch dirty movies. We ended up watching regular TV and eating Kentucky Fried Chicken—nothing was happening there. Soon afterward I asked for a divorce, which devastated our entire family. Nobody knew anything was wrong.

Feeling that everyone loathed and reviled me, I stayed away from Chad and his family. He met and married his current wife within 18 months. Chad's anger, pain, and guilt were directed at me through her and our children steadily for the next four years. I had never even had a conversation with his new wife, yet she despised me, and I felt the same way about her.

We lived one town apart, sharing custody of the kids, who lived with me during the week and visited Chad on weekends. Mondays were hell; my kids were bouncing off the wall with pain and turmoil. In 1990 we discovered that our oldest daughter was suffering from severe bulimia.

By 1993 I knew I had to get outta Dodge, and I moved to California with a new partner. At the end of August when the kids returned to visit their father before school started, he informed me by telephone that they were not returning, and he was suing me for full custody. My lawyer said that he would probably win due to his stable family situation.

For the first time in my life, I sought the help of my family about a relationship. They helped me craft a successful agreement for the care of my children and told me to go home and have a life.

I returned home and went into a state of depression for five weeks. When I came out of it, I began to heal myself doing work I loved, earning money to meet my financial obligations, and leaving the new relationship I'd hastily entered into. My girls came to visit me in my new environment and decided they wanted to stay. I asked Chad to come talk to me and to them. He did. It was the beginning.

I finally told him why I'd wanted out of our marriage. I told him how hurt and angry I was at the abuse he'd targeted at me. He understood and left the girls with me. During this time I began studying A Course in Miracles *and attending a Science of Mind church. My conversations with Chad moved from harsh to judgmental, strained to cordial, friendly to caring. Since then, Chad's new wife and I have moved beyond our anger, and we have a mutually respectful relationship.*

I have learned that it's critical to get help when communication is painful. I've also learned that my feelings are valid and deserve my attention, and sometimes concerted action. I've learned that when I don't care for myself, I can make horrific decisions; and that when I do *care for myself, miracles happen. I have also seen that under the worst of circumstances, things can and do get better. It's a matter of outlook and "in" look.*

c h a p t e r   7

An Affair to Remember

The Gift of a Third Party

"Every problem comes to you with a gift in its hands."
— Richard Bach[14]

A third party has no power to break up a healthy relationship. No one can come between you and your partner unless something has already come between you and your partner. A mate having an affair is not the cause of a breakup; it is a symptom of a breakdown in the fabric of the primary relationship. From the Big Love perspective, an affair is not a cause for condemnation of self or other; it can be the most valuable wake-up call of a lifetime.

The most important question to ask of a partner who has strayed is: *"What were you looking for that you were not finding in your primary relationship?"* There are two possible answers: (1) What he wanted was available at home, but he did not have the vision, willingness, or ability to see and claim it. Perhaps he bumped up against a fear of intimacy, or he did not have the communication skills or emotional depth to work through the issues; or (2) the home relationship simply did not have the substance for longevity, the partners were not (or are no longer) well matched, or the relationship was in some way toxic. The affair, then, was an unconscious statement that something was not right with the primary relationship.

In either case, the affair coming to light is a blessing. If the love at home was real, both partners now have the opportunity to go deeper, tell more truth, heal the issues that were troubling them, and create a partnership that transcends what both were settling for. Like a broken bone, when a fractured relationship heals, it grows stronger than it was before the break, strongest at the point where it knit.

If there was not a lot of substance to the relationship in the first place, or the partners grew irrevocably in different directions, it is probably a blessing that one partner took the step to leave. The affair set into motion a series of events that forced you to to tell more truth and ultimately freed both of you to get on with your lives. Granted, it would have been more gentle if the person who strayed came forward with direct communication, but, as the saying goes, actions speak louder than words. Our bodies communicate what our words do not, and if your wife took her body to another man's bed, she is making a statement that cannot be denied.

The only thing worse than an affair that comes to light is an affair that does *not* come to light. Yes, there was pain and upset in the aftermath of the revelation, but consider the alternative: You could have gone on for many years trudging through a half-relationship, your issues buried and your hearts weeping, never confronting the issues that were slowly killing you. Rejoice that you can now take the next step toward going deeper with each other, or moving apart. At least you have the truth on your side now.

Don't waste a moment blaming the third party. Who he is, or how she connected with you or your partner, and the details of the drama are of little importance in the face of the gifts and lessons available to you and your partner. Truth be told, it could have been anyone. If you or your partner wanted to leave, there are millions of people to run to, and if it wasn't Sally or John, it would have been Sue or Bill. The name, face, and story are far less significant than the *why*. And if there have been several or more outside partners, it *really* doesn't matter, for in such a case you can see quite clearly that the behavior was about the mate who strayed, not the third parties.

Meanwhile, the third party has her own inner work to do. Why she would choose to get involved with someone who is married or in a relationship is something she needs to look at and come to terms with. But one thing is clear: That is none of your business. The less time and energy you spend analyzing, judging, or punishing the partner who strayed or the third party, the more time and energy you will have to make the experience work on behalf of your own growth and the evolution of your relationship. Attempting to blame a third party is a tactic of distraction that takes the spotlight off of you and your partner. Bring your introspection back home, for it is there that you will find healing.

An individual who is satisfied in a relationship cannot be seduced, nor will she seek diversions. There may be momentary attractions, but if you and your partner have a Big Love and the willingness to connect in depth, the fulfillment both of you seek is present and available. Commitment is not something you create by saying words; it is an experience of the heart, and passing flirtations have no power over Big Love.

There is a principle in organic gardening that is true of relationships: Pests are less likely to attack plants that are growing in healthy soil. You can administer all kinds of pesticides or organic deterrents, but your best defense against intruders is to nourish the soil from which the plant derives its essential nutrients. Given a healthy foundation, plants develop a natural immune system superior to external additives.

Translated into human relationship, the best way to ensure a committed relationship is to keep feeding your partnership with truth, love, and intimacy. These attributes are not ones that you should expect to get from your partner (although you do); they are investments you make in your relationship. The quickest route to hell in a relationship is to expect your partner to fill your emptiness, and the most direct way to heaven is to give what you want to receive. You only receive what you give, and you receive it in the giving.

So it comes to this: you can thank and bless the third party as your teacher and awakener. Certainly this was not their intention, but it is the gift you choose to make of him or her. The third party pointed out aspects of yourself, your partner, and your relationship that you may never have discovered, or at least not for a long, long time. Bless and release the third party and get on with the business of building the kind of relationship you truly desire. Use the affair to create a Big Love with your partner that goes far beyond what shaky love offered, or use the affair to deepen loving yourself or create a more meaningful partnership with another at a later time. Everything serves, and an affair is no exception.

❧❧

Fred and Ashley:
I Became Aware of a Better Way

I used to operate through the "Big Bang" theory of relationship change. Since I was afraid to be honest and express my real feelings, I would do something so awful that my partner and I would explode apart.

Ashley and I had been working together for five years and living with each other for three. While we worked well with each other, I was becoming less content with us as primary partners. However, I couldn't tell Ashley how I was feeling because I didn't know how. I blamed her for my unhappiness, making her wrong and judging her to be somehow bad.

It was obvious to both of us that something wasn't working—so I slept with her girlfriend. I didn't premeditate this, of course, but

now in retrospect I see that I did the one thing that I knew would make her leave.

When Ashley found out, she was very hurt and angry. I pleaded with her for forgiveness, but she told me that my inability to be truthful about my real feelings needed to be rectified. So I found a psychologist, and this was perhaps the best decision I made. Before long, I discovered that my difficulty in expressing my feelings stemmed from my childhood, when I was severely punished if I was really honest. I received love and approval only when I told my parents what they wanted to hear, regardless of whether it was truthful or not.

Ashley agreed to attend some of my therapy sessions with me, and together we gained a deeper understanding of the reasons for my pattern of behavior with my partners, which had been going on for a long time before my relationship with Ashley. Through Ashley's understanding, she was able to begin to forgive me and work with me to consciously change our relationship.

My therapy with Ashley and our deepened communication was a major turning point for me. That was the beginning of the end of a pattern that had created a great deal of pain for me and others.

Since that time, Ashley and I have gone on to marry other people, and now we are both enjoying very satisfying marriages. Ashley continued to work for me for several years, we are still friends, and we have good and loving communication when we see each other. I will always be grateful to her for assisting me in becoming aware of a better way.

c h a p t e r   8

For the Sake of the Kids

Modeling Realness

"If you can give your son or daughter only one gift,
let it be enthusiasm."
— Bruce Barton

"I just feel so guilty about the kids," you sincerely confess. "The divorce has been stressful on them, and I'm afraid it will damage them emotionally for life."

The only thing that hurts children more than a divorce is to live with two parents who don't want to be together. Although a divorce is painful for everyone it touches, at least it is honest. If you can move through a divorce with kindness and mutual respect—or at least honesty and self-respect—you are offering your children a model of integrity. If, on the other hand, you stay together smiling on the outside while crying, dying, and cursing yourself and your partner on the inside, you are teaching your children to worship at the altar of fear and settle for life without love.

Children are not fooled by words or social presentation; they read feelings and energies. They listen not to the words you are saying, but to the music your soul is playing. If your soul is thriving, they soar with you; and if your soul is cringing, they die with you. The greatest legacy you can bestow upon your children is authenticity.

Unless children make a conscious choice otherwise, they tend to replicate the pattern of relationship they saw modeled by their parents. In my seminars, I have worked with many people who have recreated scenarios in which their parents were absent or abusive to each other, physically and/or emotionally. I remind them: *If you do what your parents did, you'll get the life they lived.* To ensure that your children will choose a better life than the one modeled by your parents, you must live your life in the way you hope they will live theirs.

Another form of abuse often replicated is fractured integrity: "My mother was terribly sad with my father, but she never said anything—and that is exactly the marriage I recreated." You do not have to be fighting overtly to teach your children warfare. Sometimes an internal war, never spoken but energetically indicated, is far more debilitating than overt hostility.

Illness is also a form of tacit communication. When a parent is unhappy in a marriage but avoids confronting her issues due to fear of being alone, social stigma, or religious programming, she may choose illness as an unconscious avenue of escape. The body is always communicating what the soul is experiencing, especially when fear thwarts direct communication. Thus, many people: (1) become chronically ill or fatigued; (2) create multiple accidents or emergencies that keep them bedridden or in and out of hospitals; or (3) stay immersed in therapies as a form of distraction from direct confrontation of their pain, spouse, or emotional issues. Such individuals are not simply physically sick; they are sick of their marriage and/or the way they have been living. Taken to an extreme, some people would rather die than face the issues of their relationship, and they choose death as an alternative to change. On the other hand, I have seen many people with long histories of pain and illness who choose to face and handle their marital issues head on, and experience (sometimes miraculous) improvements in their health that had previously loomed as mysterious or been diagnosed as impossible to cure.

Yet one more unhealthy model that parents offer children is distraction through addiction. Many parents who are unwilling or unable to communicate with each other directly, turn (as we noted in an earlier chapter) to alcohol, drugs, workaholism, terminal busyness, obsessive overeating, extramarital affairs, and other forms of psychic numbing. Children, who observe energy and behavior and absorb them like sponges, quickly learn the same escape routes. One morning I was speaking with the eight-year-old son of a man who runs obsessively from activity to activity, nearly to the point of exhaustion. When I asked the child what he was going to do that day, he answered, "Well, my calendar is fairly full today." We teach by our being.

Now for the good news: I have also spoken with children whose parents divorced, but when they grew up and the time came for them to make their own relationship choices, they chose on the basis of self-honoring rather than self-torture. These children established healthy adult relationships because, while their parents were going through their process, they used the experience to grow closer to themselves and their children. Even in the midst of difficult times, they offered their children a model of authenticity and aliveness. Some of the emotionally healthiest people I know grew up in families whose parents were on-again, off-again for the course of their lives. Yet these grown children had a great deal of love and respect for their parents because *their parents loved and respected themselves.* They kept passion for life as their priority and did not allow the divorce to distract them from their higher purpose as evolving souls. The form of their relationships was less important than their essence.

GLAD TO SEE THEM HAPPIER

Over the course of many years of conducting seminars and personal counseling sessions, I have heard accounts from many children who lived through the divorce of their parents. While the process was not always easy, many reported that the most painful period was living under the same roof with parents who were fighting or noncommunicative. Most of these children reported that when their parents parted, they experienced a sense of relief and release.

Here are some examples:

Jacqui, age 8: "I wish my parents would have gotten divorced long before they did; they both became much happier and nicer people when they were apart."

Jerri, age 15: "As soon as my dad left, the whole household lightened up. My dad was always angry, and my mom was always sad. Since they parted, they both seem happier. My dad has a place just a few blocks away, so we see him a lot. I think this is better for everyone."

Andrew, age 16: "Now that my parents are separated, I am really getting to know my dad. When I am with him, I get more of his attention. We have gone camping and fishing on weekends, and we never did that before. It's like I'm getting to know him for the first time."

Penny, age 21: "When my mom came to me and told me she and my dad were splitting up, she asked me, 'Are you going to be okay with this?' I told her, 'I just wish you would have done this years ago.'"

Not all children, of course, glean such positive results immediately, and I do not mean to minimize the fact that divorce can be turbulent for many children, especially younger ones. The point here is that when parting is a positive move for the parents, the expansion of their well-being is obvious to the children, who reflect it in their own well-being. The divorce, we see, is not the cause of pain, but how the parents approach it. Even the end of a marriage can be an opportunity to practice loving.

More than any words or teachings, it is the light that you are shining—or absence of it—that your children will remember. If you can find happiness in your marriage, your child will learn happiness. And if your happiness comes through traveling a different path, your child will still learn happiness. Pay less attention to the things you are doing, and more attention to the signals you are transmitting.

When parents are true to themselves,
children learn honesty, self-respect, and inner peace.

A GREATER PURPOSE

One of the most helpful ways to reframe an ended relationship is to gain a broader understanding of its purpose. There are many different reasons why people come together: friendship, romance, sexual attraction, marriage, business, and spiritual growth, to name a few. Quite often we are not aware of the purpose of a relationship until we have gotten into (or out of) it. In retrospect, we may see that the relationship had a purpose quite different from the one we originally ascribed to it.

While you may have originally come together with the expectation of being life partners, you may have realized later on that you joined, instead, in order to learn some specific lessons, stimulate each other's spiritual growth, or have a family. Ted and Lacie fell passionately in love as soon as they met, decided they were life partners, moved in together after knowing each other a few months, and then Lacie unexpectedly became pregnant. She gave birth to a beautiful boy, Lucas, and then left Ted a few years later for another man. In the years since their divorce, neither Ted nor Lacie have remarried, and they have little to do with each other. However, they both deeply love their son, whom they share custody of. Perhaps the purpose of Ted and Lacie's meeting was not to form a lifetime bond, but to bring Lucas into the world so they could experience a joy that they would not have otherwise known.

Put simply, there are three kinds of relationships: (1) *Love relationships,* in which two people truly love and appreciate each other and generally lift each other's lives to greater levels of happiness; (2) *learning relationships*, in which two people are attracted to each other in some ways, ultimately do not belong together for a lifetime, but have valuable lessons to teach and learn during the time they are together; and (3) *toxic relationships,* in which two people only hurt each other, overtly or subconsciously, by being together. Toxic relationships have no purpose except to motivate the individuals to leave and take better care of themselves.

While this classification of the three types of relationships is very general (since it is rare that a relationship falls into just one category), it does give us a helpful way to see where we stand with a partner, and empowers us to make healthy choices based on our real purpose.

If you entered into a relationship with one expectation (romance, for example) and eventually realized that your deeper purpose with your partner was friendship, spiritual support, or child-rearing; or if you thought your relationship was about sexual compatibility and it turns out to be toxic, then you have no choice but to tell the truth about your purpose. Such an admission is not a mistake at all; it is a mark of maturity and integrity to acknowledge, "This is what we thought at first, and now this is what we realize."

Such clarity will not hurt your children, but only help them. You will offer them a model of real people creating their lives as they go along. One of the most confusing and erroneous myths we have been led to believe is that parents are gods and are perfect. In the 1950s and '60s, many television shows such as *Leave It to Beaver, Father Knows Best,* and *Ozzie and Harriet* depicted parents as perfect, all-knowing paragons of virtue. Meanwhile, in real life, many of us observed parents who were alcoholic; unfaithful; physically, sexually, or emotionally abusive; living in fear-based realities; or absent. In the years since the days of the perfect media parent, movies and television have presented much more authentic models of parenting, which may be somewhat disappointing at first, but in the long run, are important to observe and understand for the sake of our healing.

The best way to prepare your child to build healthy relationships is by being authentic yourself.

So a divorce or breakup, in the Big Picture, is not a cause for shame or the failure you may have been led to believe; it may be a positive adjustment allowing you to realign your relationship with your true purpose. Let us rejoice in the process of moving closer to knowing who we truly are, and recognizing the deeper beauty of our loved ones. All of life is a coming-home process, and growing through relationship hastens us along our way.

∾∾

Jennifer and Warren:
Through the Eyes of a Child

My being 18 and pregnant in the 1970s was too much for my parents to handle. It was bad enough that I moved out after high school and was dating a hippie, but to actually want to keep this "love child" and not be wed was unthinkable. Young, scared, and broke, our marriage journey began.

When I was six months pregnant, Warren lost his job and we moved in with my parents. I was experiencing depression and some pregnancy problems. It was only through prayer that I began to feel hope, which came to life with the birth of my beautiful little girl, Nicole. This was my awakening to unconditional love, the essence of my healing.

Both of my parents were alcoholics, and I continued in their footsteps. It wasn't surprising, then, that I married a substance abuser. When I made the decision to live a substance-free life, problems really began, and my marriage became exhausting. Warren and I separated, and our relationship was on-again, off-again for several years, during which time I became pregnant and had a son. Then Warren fell back into old, self-defeating patterns, we finally separated, faced the threat of losing our home, and the unthinkable happened. Our five-year-old son was found dead, and Warren blamed me. My world collapsed. I was angry at God for taking my joy away. During all of the sadness in the marriage, my two children had become my beacons of love, my only inspiration to push on. Now my reality became unspeakably dark.

The only decision I could make to keep what little sanity I had left was to initiate divorce proceedings. After all of the unkind words, battles over who was right, feelings of abandonment by God, and my anguish at the thought that my son had died a senseless death, I sought to remove anything from my life that brought me sadness. In such grief and loss, I cried myself to sleep and went through many dark nights of the soul; I even attempted suicide once.

One night while I was crying, my daughter got out of bed to comfort me. "Why are you always crying, Mom?" she asked. I answered, "Well, baby, your brother is gone, your dad has moved out, we might lose this house, and I feel like I've lost everything." Then Nicole looked at me and spoke words of love and compassion that flowed from her heart to mine and changed my life. She said, "But Mom, you still have me."

Wow! With all the anger inside me and the changes in my life, the one force of love I knew to be true was standing right in front of me. In that moment, I could see God in the eyes of my beautiful child. It was then that I realized how unconditionally a child accepts a parent's personality. This little sage transformed the way I felt about myself and her father.

Nicole's acceptance helped me to see my ex as more than a monster. When she saw Warren, she was able to look past all of the character defects and view him as perfect—just as she pictured me. In all honesty, he loves her deeply, and I now realize that the problem was not just him as a father; it was the way we lived our relationship.

When I told Warren about that experience, it was the beginning of healing ten years of marriage disappointment. Because I was never taught self-love or self-worth, I didn't know how to be gentle with myself. The more I shared this story, the more I forgave myself.

My new goal was to feel joy again and not settle for just moving beyond grief and sadness. But how was this to happen? I looked at my young mentor again and decided to see life through the eyes of a child. Every time I asked Nicole, "What's new?" or "What's good?" her response brought me right back to the present moment. I began sharing many of the little stories with Warren that he now missed hearing on a daily basis. Then the most amazing thing happened—we began to laugh together again. And we spent time together as a family.

One day Nicole asked if her dad and I were ever going to get back together again. When I said that I didn't believe so, she said, "Good." When I asked her why, she told me that we are both happier and more fun to be around now that we didn't live together. And now, even after all these years, our story continues to grow in love and beauty. Recently we both had the honor of walking our little girl down the aisle and placing her beside a wonderful life partner.

The lessons from these three great teachers will last me many lifetimes. I now thank God for my ex, who taught me to respect myself and others, and to know that relationships can continue even when they change form. I honor my intuitive little son and spiritual guide, whose short time with me helped me understand death and not be afraid of it. And my heart will always be grateful to Nicole, the special little child who taught me to embrace life and find beauty in the present moment. These dear friends and teachers have shown me how to immerse myself in love, joy, and a passion for life beyond measure.

Goood-Bye for Good

Rituals to Cut the Cord

"There are two ways you are empowered by any endeavor:
First, when you enter into it with a whole heart;
and second, when you let it go with a whole heart."
— Alan Cohen

O ne of the great tragedies of Western civilization is its absence of meaningful rituals. While the lives of ancient and indigenous people were enriched by ceremonies that marked the milestones of birth, adulthood, spiritual initiation, marriage, and death, our modern world is sadly bereft of healthy rites to honor important personal transitions.

In our culture, the ritual that is given the most attention is marriage. For as long as a year in advance of the ceremony, the betrothed and their families often make elaborate preparations, incorporating multifarious prescribed customs such as courting, proposal, the bestowal of a ring, lavish event planning, a bridal shower, and a bachelor party. When the wedding day arrives, the bride and groom are separated, they don traditional vestments, engage in superstitious practices ("Something borrowed, something blue"), seat their guests on appropriate sides of the church, signify a best man and matron of honor, dress bridesmaids and ushers in coordinated costumes, march to a traditional tune, stand before a strictly chosen clergyman, utter formal vows, exchange rings, publicly kiss to the applause of tearful spectators, exit to a conventional anthem, and brave a shower of rice, which symbolizes fertility.

The wedding reception, too, is replete with protocol, such as a receiving line, the first dance by the newlyweds, the tinkling of glasses by guests, a toast, husband and wife feeding each other cake, the removal of the garter, and the bride tossing the bouquet. The newlyweds dash off to their car decorated by friends with soap-writing and tin cans, the procession of guests' autos honks its way through town, and the couple honeymoons at an exotic destination resort where the groom carries the bride over the threshold and the marriage is consummated with their first (ahem) sexual encounter. Surely in our society there is no other ritual with so many detailed prescriptions.

Does it not seem strange, then, that when the most glorified event in a couple's life runs its course and ends, it simply dribbles into ignominy in the wake of a gut-wrenching legal wrestling match? Perhaps the greatest unspoken sorrow of divorce is that it is not honored as a significant turning point, placed in a higher context, acknowledged by the community in a spirit of support, and offered to God for blessings and encouragement for two individuals who are about to begin a new life—newer in many ways than the marriage.

Conscious parting requires as much attention, care, and support as a wedding—perhaps more so. Family, friends, and community came together in a time of joy to uphold the couple as they set out on their marriage; now, as they are parting (often amidst a sense of pain, loss, and grief), the couple needs love, support, and the blessings of their community more than ever. Instead, divorce is more often gossiped about than addressed directly, and sometimes friends and co-workers deny it almost entirely in word, emotion, and deed.

Rather than approaching divorce with a sense of stoic resilience, unspoken rage, emotional tailspin, or quiet embarrassment, it should be approached with a sense of blessing, empowerment, and even celebration. And for many people who have a hard time accepting love and support from others, one of the hidden blessings of a divorce is the opportunity to learn that people are really there for you, and to receive their love.

In our culture, the only divorce ceremony is the signing of a legal document. If you have ever had divorce papers placed before you to sign, you know how many emotions that one signature dredges up—from deep sadness, to guilt, to anger, to a sense of completion, to joy and freedom. These feelings arise because you are not just signing a piece of paper; you are signifying the end of an important phase of your life and the beginning of another. For many people, signing the divorce agreement calls forth some of the deepest feelings and emotional processing of their lives. Such a momentous turning point not only significantly impacts you, but equally affects your spouse, and if you have children, it marks one of the most pivotal moments of their childhood.

We need to hold such an auspicious situation in the clearest light possible, and bring to bear upon it as much love and consciousness as we can. The occasion calls not for a quick "getting it over with," but sincere attention, contemplation, sincerity, and a prayerful ceremony to anchor it in a spiritual context and call for support from a Higher Power.

In the absence of a meaningful, societally sanctioned parting ritual, many couples are creating their own. I received a beautiful letter from Bob and Alexandra, a couple who had been married for many years, lovingly announcing their parting and enclosing a copy of the divorce ceremony they had co-created:

We come together today to celebrate our relationship and commit to continuing to love each other always. We acknowledge that our lives have changed, and while our personal paths have taken different directions, we wish to end our marriage on a note of honor and appreciation. We declare that all is well, and affirm that the God who has guided our relationship for 21 years will continue to guide us as individuals and as friends.

We declare our intention to enjoy a lifelong relationship of mutual support and understanding, so we may participate kindly in each other's lives and in the lives of our beautiful children.

I hereby release you, (Bob) (Alexandra), to follow your personal path and fulfill the destiny you choose, with my deepest appreciation for the love, kindness, and support you have continually shown me, and for walking by my side during both times of joy and challenge. I thank you for being a good (father) (mother) for our children. I also acknowledge you for the many gifts, kindnesses, and favors you have shown me in word, thought, and deed, which I may not have acknowledged at the time.

So go in peace with my blessings, (Bob) (Alexandra), and know that my love and highest wishes go with you wherever you go.

> *May the peace of God go with you.*
> *May the love of God fill your heart.*
> *May the truth of God bring forth your sacred dreams,*
> *Now and forevermore.*

Although Bob and Alexandra's ceremony would have been considered an oddball event not too long ago, more and more couples are finding the courage and creativity to honor each other and their separation. Whether you are in the process of breaking up or have already done so, you may want to consider creating a ceremony that marks your transition. Such a rite, done with pure intent, can be a powerful turning point in your relationship and your life. Here are some suggestions for the creation of a meaningful parting ritual:[16]

1. Be sure both partners enter into it consensually. The very
    agreement to conduct the ceremony will empower both
    of you and accomplish much on behalf of the relation-
    ship you intend to transform. (If your partner does not
    wish to co-create such a ritual, suggestions are given in a
    later chapter for you to create your own.)

2. Choose a neutral place and time that is peaceful and
    inspiring for both of you. A park, beach, mountaintop, or
    sanctuary works well; the house or bedroom in which
    you have a great deal of history and residual pain is not a
    good choice.

3. Write a script that is meaningful for you. This is your
    chance to speak from your heart in your own words. You
    may co-create a script or each write your own. You may
    also choose to speak extemporaneously. Writing before-
    hand will assist you to focus and stay true to what you
    really want to say.

4. Conduct your ritual alone or with a few supportive
    friends as witnesses. I do not suggest you make a big
    party out of it; several beloved ones (if any) will serve to
    anchor your commitment as a public declaration. You
    can decide whether or not it is appropriate for your chil-
    dren to attend. In general, older children will fare better
    than younger ones.

5. Keep your script or statements short and positive. Do
    not dredge up pain or open emotional wounds. You have
    probably spent a great deal of time processing your feel-
    ings, and want to get on with your life. This ritual has
    one purpose: to openly acknowledge the completion of
    your relationship as it was, and honor the beginning of a
    new phase for both of you. This is not the time to ana-

lyze, blame, apologize, or make anyone or anything wrong. It is a time to celebrate the rightness of what you are doing.

6. Include these important elements in your ceremony:

    • Gratitude for the relationship as a whole
    • Thanks for the specific gifts you and your partner have brought each other
    • A clear acknowledgment that the relationship as it was, is now complete
    • A vision for your relationship as you would now like it to be
    • Blessings and good wishes for the new life to come for both of you

7. Incorporate symbolic objects. For example:

    • Remove the rings you once wore
    • Burn a piece of paper with writing that symbolized your marriage or relationship
    • Cast the ashes of the paper or cast flowers to the garden, wind, river, or sea
    • Turn over some earth, symbolizing the changes in your lives, and plant a seed symbolizing your new life
    • Give each other an inexpensive gift (or object from nature) representing your new direction

8. Finish with a short, clear affirmation, such as: *"We now agree and declare that all past vows are null and void, our relationship as it was, is complete, and we free each other to pursue our personal paths of joy."*

Once you complete your parting ritual, you will be amazed at how much more alive and empowered you will feel. While you enjoyed a short or long time of reward in your relationship, from the point you began to emotionally separate, you probably trudged down a long, rocky road to get to this point. Your parting ceremony signifies the end of the painful trek, and the beginning of a new era for both of you.

FORGING AHEAD WITH CONVICTION

Strong decisions call forth everything unlike themselves, and saying good-bye to a significant relationship will surely bring up any resistance you have to it. Just as getting married probably called forth your fears of changing your life, saying good-bye will do the same. In preparation for your ritual, take time to contemplate, write in your journal, and discuss any fears and considerations with someone who supports you. If you are on healthy terms with your partner, share your feelings openly with him or her. If not, confide in a friend or counselor. Do not attempt to play Superman or Superwoman, hide or bottle up your emotions, and do it all yourself. Untying the knot with your partner is a significant life change, and you will do well to open up so you can receive as much support as you can.

It is extremely important that you become as clear as possible on how your new relationship will differ from the old one. Some common questions couples must answer are: Will we still be friends? Do we feel comfortable seeing each other in social situations? Is dating each other appropriate? Can we still have sex? Should we just sever our activities for now and give each other some time to regroup and figure out what we will do as individuals? Will we still spend time together as a family? Will we tell each other about our new partners?

You will have to come to terms with such questions; if you do not, any ambiguity will come back to haunt you until you make the choice that works for you and live it. It is quite natural for you to start out being unclear; discovering the answers to these questions is an important part of the process. Eventually, however, you must make a stand and forge ahead with conviction.

One of the most self-defeating errors that couples make in the process of parting is to attempt to carry on aspects of romance after the intimacy and commitment have passed. It is important for you to really be on the bus or really get off the bus. If you try to straddle two worlds, you will be torn in half like a wishbone. In this situation, your only salvation is commitment—either really do the relationship, or really do not. If you dive back in, you will go deeper, and if you dive out, you will both be free to find greater fulfillment on your own or with new partners. Ultimately, the only safe place to dive is authenticity.

One day I sat on a beach with my friend Arlene and a couple, Earl and Cheryl, who were going through a divorce. The couple's conversation was dotted with thinly veiled emotional jabs and sarcastic barbs, which I found quite irksome. Although Earl and Cheryl were in the midst of divorce proceedings, they were considering buying a piece of property together, situated about a three-hour drive from where we sat. "Would you two like to take a ride with us to look at the property?" Earl asked.

My immediate thought was, *No way I want to spend the next seven hours in your crossfire!* Attempting to be diplomatic, I answered, "Thank you, but I have other plans." (Anything *is a better plan,* I thought to myself.) Arlene, however, offered a more honest answer: "I am feeling pretty uncomfortable with the animosity you are projecting toward each other, and I don't think I could be in that atmosphere with you for a long time." I was stunned by Arlene's directness, which I profoundly respected. Earl and Cheryl, however, were not put off at all; they were well aware of their dynamics, and they told Sharon they understood. The couple went off on their trip and later plowed their way through a complicated divorce (compounded by Cheryl getting pregnant and having another child). And I learned that driving south while you are heading north will not get you where you really want to go.

If you are breaking up, don't attempt to continue your sexual relationship. While sleeping together may be tempting in the face of the emotional upset you're going through, sex will ultimately not soothe the hurt, but merely exacerbate it. When you make love, you open emotionally and psychically to your partner. Such deep feelings require a safe and supportive context. You may enjoy a night of excitement and warmth, but when you both wake up and attempt to carry on with separate lives, one or both of you will feel empty and unfulfilled. Then you will be right back in the thick of the issues that led to your breakup, only more so. You will do better to focus instead on healing any emotional wounds or distress. If you choose to stay together, your sex will be infinitely more meaningful and rewarding. And if you choose to part, you are free to redirect your sexual energies toward a relationship in which you can feel whole after sex, rather than empty.

While setting boundaries isn't always fun, it will help you immensely in your process of parting, and ultimately accelerate the new friendship you seek to build. You can set boundaries with love, kindness, and mutual respect. You are setting them not to hurt each other, but to support each other in both having what you really want.

"Good-bye" doesn't mean "I don't love you." In many cases it means, "I love you and myself so much that I am unwilling to continue on a path that is hurting both of us. I care about us enough to give us both the space to nurture our hearts." Then you can meet anew at a deeper level, or go on to love yourself or another in a way that fulfills your dreams rather than destroying them.

Richard and Jane:
She Carefully Buried My Ring

When Jane and I agreed to a divorce, it was because the strategies we had tried for over a year to restore vitality to our fading marriage had failed. It was obvious—though painful—that we simply did not belong together any longer as man and wife.

We certainly had never anticipated this day when, glowing with love, we had pronounced our vows, promising that everything would last forever. "Everything" turned out to include things we hadn't counted on, and "forever" lasted three and a half years.

Eventually we came to terms with the ending of our marriage. Not fully—that took years of shedding illusions and acknowledging "the facts." But we cried and laughed together. We forgave each other. We began to see the lessons we had learned so that failure could begin to look—if not feel—more like victory.

We realized that we needed a ceremony to mark the completion of our marriage. After all, the wedding ceremony had been a planned event. Why not our divorce? We spent time discussing our separation ceremony. One afternoon a few days later, we "got divorced."

It was a private ceremony. We started with a meditative time on cushions by the fireplace. We recalled the best and the worst of our times together, the way we met, and the firsts: first kiss, first sex, the proposal, meetings with parents, and so on. We also confronted the worsts: the dishonesty, the broken promises, the aborted plans and dreams. We cried buckets.

We ate fine Belgian chocolates and drank expensive champagne from two exquisite crystal glasses, a prized wedding gift. When we were finished reminiscing, we hurled our glasses (which represented to us the most precious "things" we owned) into the fireplace. They shattered into a thousand shards. Then we left the house and walked to a nearby forest, our sanctuary for several years. Our favorite trail led to a secluded clearing. We took the wedding rings from each other's fingers and held them in an open palm. In turn, we faced each other—eye to teary eye—and spoke our separation vows. We acknowledged the pleasure and pain of our friendship and marriage, and vowed to sever our wedded connection but strengthen our friendship.

As I finished speaking, an immense rush of energy flooded through my body, with a mixture of grief and joy. It lifted my arm, and in an unpremeditated act, I hurled Jane's wedding ring off into the trees. When she completed her vows, she bent to the forest floor and carefully buried my ring. She whispered, "This ring was a symbol of our connection in marriage. Now it can be a symbol of walking this same Earth, as friends forever."

Our separation ceremony did not complete everything we needed to do to successfully make the transition from man and wife to good friends. That has taken years. We live thousands of miles apart now and see each other infrequently. When we get together, we still do some processing, but we feel liberated from guilt and judgment—we're separate yet somehow still together. We know that being so conscious and deliberate about our breakup helped. I guess that there are times in our lives when ritual can accomplish what nothing else can.

chapter 10

Glad We Talked

Communication Heals

"Ever has it been that love knows not its own depth until the hour of separation."

— Kahlil Gibran

When I was in graduate school, I dated a lovely coed named Marge. After several months, Marge and I recognized that our relationship was not going where we wanted, and we parted on less than amicable terms. Feeling uncomfortable with the way we broke up, I stuffed my emotions and avoided communicating with her.

One night I saw Marge unexpectedly at a party, and I realized that I wasn't going to be able to dodge her anymore. She invited me to sit down and have a talk, and afterwards I felt quite relieved and at peace with Marge and our relationship.

A few years later, I learned that Marge had been killed in an auto accident. Upon hearing the news, I felt shocked and saddened by the loss of my friend. Looking back on our relationship, I was deeply grateful that we had said good-bye on a loving, positive note. It was a blessing that we had met at that party and chose to communicate.

Often relationships end on a sour note, and both parties go their ways—frustrated, angry, and upset. You can probably think of at least one former partner whom you would rather not talk to. The way healing works, however, is that the one you would prefer *not* to talk to is usually the one you *most* need to talk to, or at least find a way to hold in greater peace in your heart. If such a person has hurt or irritated you so profoundly, there is a wealth of transformation available as you hold the relationship up to a greater light. So your ex is not your enemy, but your enlightener, pointing you directly to the mother lode of unaddressed energy that will lead you to freedom when you face and master your unresolved issues.

As divine beings, our nature is love, and we cannot be fully at peace as long as we nurse bitterness or resentment.

Releasing the past is not a moral issue, but a psychological principle; if you allow your life force to be undermined by animosity, the universe will not let you rest until your desire for peace waxes stronger than your propensity for alienation. The moment you make the choice for healing, you liberate tremendous freedom, clarity, aliveness, and creativity. You must plug the psychic leak and redirect your energy toward creating what you really want in your life.

The more intimate your interaction with your former partner, the greater the opportunity for transformation. The deeper the pain, the higher you will fly as you resolve it. All the emotional energy you have invested is like bouncing a rubber ball against the floor. As it impacts, all the force that has been imbued into it reverses direction, and you mobilize tremendous power for change. Making the choice for love lifts you to unprecedented heights of personal fulfillment.

Author Og Mandino[16] suggests a powerful exercise to improve the quality of any relationship: *Imagine that you will never see this person again after midnight tonight.*

If you were told that you could have ten minutes with your ex, after which you would never see her again, how would you use the time? The ego, or separated self, might use this time to vent your unspoken rage and really give her a piece of your mind. But is that how you would really like to leave the relationship unto eternity? The heart, on the other hand, would use this precious moment for healing. Perhaps you would say good-bye in a loving way and thank her for your time together. Perhaps you would want to share with her the unspoken thoughts or feelings you withheld in fear. Perhaps you would want to just look into her eyes for one last time and embrace her. Perhaps you would wish her well and bid her Godspeed in her journey.

One of the blessings of impending death (and all endings) is that it forces us to take stock of the life that preceded it. Many people have told me that in the face of a family member's imminent passing, they communicated all the things they wish they had said years earlier. You do not have to wait until someone is about to die before you deliver your truth to them. You have the power to reach out to them now and give both of you the gift of many years of feeling connected—or at least a sense of peace and relief—before either of you departs this world. What a beautiful and attractive alternative to feeling separate and alone! When you deliver your message of caring, most likely the other person will respond in kind; and even if he does not, your soul will be at peace, knowing that you were true to yourself and that you made your offering with a pure heart.

I saw a television news story about a New York family whose father was killed by a crazed gunman who opened up fire on the Long Island Railroad. A reporter asked the man's widow, "What is your most cherished memory of your husband?" The wife smiled and answered, "On the morning of the day he was killed, I stood at the door as he left the house, kissed him good-bye, and told him, 'I love you' just as I did every day when he went to work. Now I'm so glad those were the last words I spoke to him."

We never really know if we will see any particular person again. That is why it is important that we be as complete as possible with all our relationships. Take a moment now to close your eyes and scan your mind and heart to see if there is anyone with whom you feel incomplete, or to whom you would like to communicate more. Observe whose face pops into your mind. Then consider what you would really like to say to this person that would bring peace, relief, or joy to both of you.

Then go about your soul's business, and do what you need to do to be more complete with this significant person. It might be the most important conversation of your life.

THE FINAL MESSAGE

"But there's no way I could tell that so-and-so I love him; that's not that way I feel, and I have to be honest," you sincerely object. The goal of real communication is not to say an artificial "I love you"; it is to come to a place of resolution. If you need to express or clear negative emotions to get to resolution, then that is what you need to do. And if entering into the abode of silence within you will give you the clarity you seek, that is what you need to do. If your intention is truly to heal, you will do so, no matter what route you take.

Saying "I love you" does not necessarily mean "I feel romantic with you," "I want to sleep with you," or "I want to rekindle our relationship." We have equated many things with love, many of which have little to do with real love. The "I love you" we are looking for is a statement that you appreciate and respect this person and desire their happiness and good. If you can say this with sincerity to your ex, you are well on your way to the release you seek, and to creating a better relationship in the future.

Werner Erhard conducted an experiment in which he gathered circles of people who knew each other and asked each group member to take a turn sitting in the center of the circle. Then each person in the circle expressed a feeling about the person in the center. At first, the speakers focused on their negative feelings, such as "I don't like your sarcastic jokes," or "I'm upset about the time you left work early and I got stuck with the job." The speakers kept taking turns over and over until they had all spoken all of their feelings.

The experiment showed consistently that nearly every speaker's statements became more and more positive and appreciative, until their final statement was "I love you." After these people had released their upsets and expressed their complaints, all that was left was love.

All of our interactions are avenues through which
we seek to express and receive love.

While presenting a seminar to a group of teenagers and young adults at a church, I asked, "Who among you has someone in your life that you would like to say 'I love you' to, but have not done so because you've been afraid?"

Several dozen people raised their hands.

"I would like to give you an opportunity to express your feelings," I told the audience. "I will now offer ten of you five minutes each on the telephone, courtesy of my calling card, to call someone and tell them 'I love you' for the first time, or the first time in a long time."

Eagerly, ten participants took me up on my offer. One by one, they went into the minister's office and made their important calls. A little while later, each came back to the assembly glowing, and reported wonderful experiences.

One fellow, however, returned looking rather serious, and he did not make a public report. I was concerned that he had not had a successful experience. I did not have the opportunity to speak with him, and when the seminar was over, this young man remained in my thoughts.

Then, several weeks later, I received a letter from him, including this account:

While I have a capacity to receive love from others, I struggle with giving. When you made the offer, I chose my father, a man whom I have always loved and admired. My parents were divorced when I was young, and so my relationship with my father was only what I knew of him on certain weekends. I had struggled for resolution for as long as I can remember. My answer was simple: I wanted to tell my father that I loved him.

From out of nowhere I felt a strong sense of courage like never before in my life. As I dialed the number, I felt swept away by my emotions, but I was still driven by my long-awaited desire. As my father answered the phone, my emotions got the best of me, but I was able to tell him for the first time since the divorce how much I appreciate him.

I wasn't expecting anything in return, but what I got meant so much to me. He shared his feelings with me, something I've never heard him do. I felt so warm inside, and I could literally feel the weight lift off my shoulders.

It occurred to me that all this time I was looking for ways or excuses to tell my father how I felt, but it was there all along. Thank you for giving me the chance to discover that I am capable of giving love, and that when I do, the rewards are tremendous!

INTENTION MAKES THE DIFFERENCE

The crucial factor behind all communication is *intention*. The results you glean will not come from the words you speak, but from the goals you are holding. If your intention is clear, you can speak all the wrong words and you will succeed; if your intention is muddled or ambiguous, you can say all the right things but walk away frustrated.

Before communicating, check in with your gut, and explore your real intentions. If your intention is to heal and come to a place of peace and harmony, then go for it. If, however, you still feel like a villain or victim, want to be right, or feel that communicating now would plunge you into just another repeat of the ongoing argument you've been having for a long time, you would do better to keep working on yourself until your intention is purified.

One further note: In some cases, it is better not to attempt to communicate physically. If someone is extremely angry, volatile, or unstable, and an attempt to communicate would only aggravate the situation and cause more problems, you do better to let that person be, and speak to him or her through your mind, heart, and spirit. (We will describe this practice in a later chapter.)

The truth is a two-edged sword; you can use it to heal or to maim. Be careful that the truth you tell leads you to greater release and not more entanglement. *A Course in Miracles* reminds us, "When you want only love, you will see nothing else." The moment you are ready to accept healing, it will come. It is not a sin to feel separate from someone; this is quite normal in human relations. But it is a sin (self-inflicted nonsense) to write someone off as unreachable and allow your relationship to wither.

Every human being is a precious gift, and every relationship is holy, with infinite potential for love, joy, and awakening. To talk yourself out of love is to miss the only treasure that will fulfill you. And to capture the delight of reconnecting with someone you love is to claim the happiness your heart truly longs to feel.

❦❦
Tara and Ben:
We Really Did Love Each Other

I didn't feel love at first sight with Ben. He seemed too opinionated to me. And he had such a strong personality. Besides, I was engaged to another man.

I met Ben in 1973 when I was working as a waitress in an Italian restaurant in New Jersey. He came in often after work and kept asking me out. Finally, I said okay to a lunch invitation—then he asked me to fly with him in his plane to Martha's Vineyard for lunch! I had suspected he was well off, but this was a surprise. It was a fairy-tale afternoon. For our second date, he asked me to bring along my five-year-old son, Michael. After much thought, I broke my engagement, and Ben and I began dating seriously.

One night Ben took me to dinner at the restaurant where we'd met. He handed me an envelope with two round-trip plane tickets to Germany, where I grew up. I was stunned! I hadn't seen my family since I left there at the age of 15 in 1957. The trip, he said, was a chance for me to have my mother meet her grandson, and for me to think over if I would like to marry him. He told me to stay as long as I wanted, and that my ticket and Michael's were on open return. Michael and I returned after three weeks and numerous transatlantic phone calls. Ben and I set an October date for our wedding.

Ben told me he had bought me an engagement present while I was away, and he wanted to show it to me. He had me sit in his car and handed me a blindfold to wear. He drove a while, stopped, got me out of the car, and removed my blindfold. Before me was the most beautiful house I had ever seen—and in a fabulous neighborhood! For our honeymoon we flew to the Great Exuma Islands. I became pregnant on those romantic isles, and nine months later our son Barry was born.

In time, Ben's very successful business met some serious set-backs. He lost his company, and we had to sell our wonderful house. We moved into a small home on a horse farm in another part of the state. We were there for two years while Ben rebuilt his business. He was not happy. He had been an orphan who had lived on farms for his keep, and now this seemed to be déjà vu. Ben had also expected that I could fill his needs, and we learned that that doesn't work in a relationship. We began to have a lot of arguments, which were directly related to Ben's business pressures.

We lacked good communication, as Ben did not express his anger in words. It was while we lived on the horse farm that Ben first hit me. The abuse occurred during heavy business challenges accompanied by emotional disturbance. He hated himself.

Still, Ben built a strong business again. Then, amid the pressures of constructing a new factory, his previously moderate drinking and smoking increased. Our little differences grew enormous, and we saw a marriage counselor. Then I found out he was seeing other women.

One day Ben told me that he thought we'd be happier apart, and I became very bitter. I told the judge he was a wife beater. We put our home on the market, and Ben sued me for custody of Barry—and got it. For two years we barely spoke. If anybody ever hated anybody, I hated Ben. Later we both commented on how angry we had felt that we couldn't make our life together work. There was potentially such a good life for us! Instead, we had a bitter divorce and experienced two years of resentment.

Again Ben lost his business. He was living in a rented efficiency and working as a security guard. Then he got sick and had brain surgery for a cancerous tumor. Since Ben was a Navy Seal veteran of the Korean War, where he had earned a Purple Heart, he entered a veterans' hospital. He had no business, no car, and no spare funds. My niece offered to let Ben live rent-free in a family home she owned. I had gotten a very good job looking after an *elderly couple who gave me a car, which I gave to Ben. I could now afford to buy my own car.*

More health challenges plagued Ben. He became diabetic and had problems with his legs, but he continued to work full time as a security guard. A man with a master's degree in chemistry and a history of astonishing business successes, failures, and comebacks—now a security guard. During this time, Barry lived with me, and I wanted Ben to relinquish his custody.

Instead, when his health improved, Ben made Barry the focus of his life. He encouraged his son to go for a football scholarship at a major Midwestern university, and he got it! Ben moved there himself and got a job in a plant similar to those he had owned and managed. He was there for his son, his only natural child. He had loved and raised Michael, too, and Michael also called him Dad.

In March of 1996, Ben had a major stroke at age 62. I rushed to where Barry and Ben were. Ben was mostly paralyzed, couldn't talk, and shook his head "no" when anything was offered.

Barry became Ben's legal guardian. Ben could not swallow, but his brain was still sharp. The medical technicians tried to get him to feed through a tube, but he ripped it out. They moved him to another hospital where he was put on an apparatus that prevented him from removing any tubes. Two days later, Ben had a second stroke and died. We were grateful for God's mercy and grateful for having known Ben, in both the good and bad times.

All of us grew so much closer in the last years. Ben and Barry and I all knew that it is love and caring, not the material things or the crutches like alcohol or cigarettes, that make a person happy, that make a family. Rich and poor, sick and healthy— we'd experienced it all together and apart. Life dealt us lessons, and we learned. We all really did, and always will, love each other very much.

chapter 11

The Main Thing

Keeping Love First

"It is only with the heart that one can see rightly.
What is essential is invisible to the eye."
— from *The Little Prince*,[17]
by Antoine de Saint-Exupery

While visiting my friend's gift shop, I discovered a T-shirt proclaiming a most profound truth:

The main thing is to keep the main thing the main thing.

But before you can keep the main thing the main thing, you have to know what the main thing is. A divorce or painful breakup is a powerful way to put you in touch with what the main thing is.

Jerry, a sculptor from Eugene, Oregon, learned about the main thing when his partner moved out:

When Martine left, we faced the onerous task of decid-
ing what to do with the house we had purchased together. I
wanted to keep the house, and we agreed that I would buy

out Martine's share of it. But when we tried to determine the value of the house, we hit a wall. The house was an unusual one in a country area where no two properties are alike, and the real estate market was in a boom. Martine thought the house was worth more, and I thought it was worth less. We grappled over negotiations for a while, which were strained under the emotional issues surrounding our breakup. Finally, our communication broke down. "I refuse to speak to you directly," Martine stated coldly. "I want an offer in writing, or else I will get a lawyer."

I could not believe that we had come to such odds. During our relationship, we had enjoyed excellent communication and supported each other very lovingly. Now this woman with whom I had been so close was speaking to me as if I were an enemy. I felt deeply troubled by the distance that had grown between us, and I feared that we had opened a can of worms we would not be able to put the lid on. I turned to God for help, praying deeply and consistently that we would come to a fair and amiable resolution.

During a time of meditation, the name "Lawrence Brown" popped into my mind. Lawrence was a man I had met just a few times briefly several years earlier; I remembered him telling me that he was in real estate. Perhaps, I thought, he could give me some advice on how to work out a deal that would take care of both Martine and myself.

I found Lawrence's number in the directory and got him on the phone. "Lawrence, you're in real estate, aren't you?" I began.

"Actually, I'm not," he answered. "I'm an interior designer."

I felt embarrassed. "Well, I guess I made a mistake. Sorry to bother you."

"Tell my why you called; perhaps I can help you anyway."

Still feeling a little foolish, I laid out the facts of my

predicament with Martine. When I finished, Lawrence told me, "I know why you called."

"Why is that?"

"I went through a similar situation in my divorce a few years ago. My wife was extremely demanding in our settlement, asking for way more than I felt was fair. We also hit a wall, and our lawyers were squaring off."

"So how did you resolve it?"

"I thought about our marriage and the kind of relationship I wanted to continue to have with her. We had been married for 13 years, during which we shared many beautiful experiences and two wonderful daughters. I didn't want to see all that marred by an ugly fight over money. So in the name of harmony, our children, and our future, I decided to give her what she was asking for. The moment I let go of struggling, I felt peace.

"And do you know what?" Lawrence went on. "I don't regret it one bit. The difference between what I originally offered and what I ended up settling for has come back to me a hundred times over in my business. Now we have a good connection, our kids are happy, and everything worked out fine."

I breathed a deep sigh of relief as I thanked Lawrence for the answer I was looking for, and hung up the phone with a softened heart. While I thought I was looking for financial advice, I was really needing spiritual wisdom. God had truly answered my prayers by planting Lawrence's name in my mind. Out of the many thousands of people I know, including scores of Realtors and business people, I consider it a miracle that I chose to follow a hunch and call the one casual acquaintance who had lived the answer I needed to hear.

The next time I talked to Martine, I made her an offer close to what she was asking.

"Really?" she answered. "You're not going to deduct . . ."
"No, that's my offer."
Then, to my amazement, Martine made me a counter offer in my favor, and offered to buy some equipment from me at a higher price than I could have gotten on the open market. In a few minutes, we came to a mutual agreement in which I refinanced the house and she held a second mortgage. Subsequently, my business prospered, and I paid off her mortgage in a fraction of the time we agreed upon. Now I own the house, she got what she felt was a fair return on her investment, and we have both gone on with our lives while holding each other in loving regard.

People going through a divorce or breakup use four issues as political footballs: children, money, possessions, and time. Because we attach emotional significance to these issues, we withhold them as our way of saying, "I don't feel loved by you, so I will hurt you by withholding something you want." We turn a relationship into a bargaining game, which hooks the other person in their most vulnerable place and leads to a terrible cycle of attack, defense, counterattack, frustration, pain, and confusion. In the end, nobody wins.

We cannot afford to place things before love, or put dissension before kindness. We know the awful psychological ramifications that children experience when they become bargaining chips in their parents' tugs-of-war. It's just not worth it.

When we make win-win our highest priority, somehow things work out for everyone. This does not mean that you need to agree to anything that is grossly unfair, or just roll over and let your former partner hurt you. It simply means that when dealing with "stuff," we must remember that Spirit is more important than matter. Leo Buscaglia noted that "we were meant to love people and use things—but we end up loving things and using people."

Do your best not to throw your partner out of your heart. Tell the truth, ask for what you want, stand for what you sincerely believe, but don't cast your former beloved as your enemy. You both want to live more rewarding lives, and you can really help each other if you choose.

THE POWER OF ATTRACTION

While a seminar sponsor was driving me from an airport to the auditorium where I was to lecture, I told her, "I like your car."

"Thank you," Harriet answered. "My husband wants it as part of the divorce we are going through. I fought with him about it, since I brought the car into the marriage. But then I figured that I got the car by right of my consciousness, and so I can always get another one. If I had the power to attract such a car, he could take six of them from me, but I would just keep manifesting them. So I told him he could have it."

Harriet was making use of a principle that most people do not understand, and rarely apply consciously. It is called the *Law of Attraction.* What we have comes to us not by chance, circumstance, or external conditions; we have it because we attract it to us by our readiness and willingness to receive it, as we express through our thoughts, feelings, and actions. Things "belong" to us not just because we paid for them, but because we love them, we generate mental and emotional energy toward them, and they match who and where we are on our path. This explains why some people are successful in business no matter what they do, and others keep trying to claw their way out of a hole. A success-minded individual may lose everything or change careers, and within a short time will again manifest all that she lost, and more. Meanwhile, others set out on a different get-rich-quick scheme every other week and end up losing more with each foray. Such a person may blame his failures on a million different external causes, but the truth is that he has not developed the consciousness to attract what he wants and keep it. Abundance-oriented people, on the other hand, cannot keep their good from them.

It is useless to fight over things. If you want and need something that you shared, you will have it, either by keeping the original object, or getting another one. The Law of Attraction also applies to relationship partners. If someone leaves you, it is foolish to bemoan the loss. *Rejection is protection.* You can manifest another partner with even more desirable qualities. I remember being afraid to break up with a relationship partner, telling myself that I would never find anyone else with such wonderful looks, intelligence, or sensitivity. Then, lo and behold, before too long I met someone else whom I appreciated even more. "Not enough to go around" and "poor me" are tricks of the frightened mind, and we only hurt ourselves when we play small. We have the power to manifest all that we want and need when we know who we are and we put universal principles into action on our own behalf.

THE ACTIVE INGREDIENT

While reading the ingredients on a tube of toothpaste, I noticed that there was one chemical (out of about a dozen) designated as "the active ingredient." While all the other ingredients give the toothpaste color, taste, texture, and fluff, the active ingredient is the one that actually gets your teeth clean. Without it, the toothpaste would look and taste great, but it would be utterly useless.

> *The active ingredient in a relationship, breaking up, and all of life is love.*

If you put Big Love first, all answers will make themselves known to you, and you will be clearly guided as to how to handle every situation as it arises. If you drop love to a lower rung on your priority list, you will fall prey to fear, feel lost and confused, and act ineffectively. You may be able to power-trip, manipulate, or intimidate your former partner so you can get what you think you want, ineffectively. You may be able to power-trip, manipulate, or intimidate your former partner so you can get what ou think you want, but what you get through ego-driven tactics is not what you really want. Is it really the home entertainment center that you desire, or would you rather keep your soul?

The miracle of love is that when you keep Big Love the main thing, you will likely get the home entertainment center as well. It may come from your marriage, or it may come in another way— it doesn't really matter. What really matters is that you can sleep at night and know that you chose joining rather than conflict. Then you will enjoy the deep satisfaction of knowing that you've kept the main thing the main thing.

❧❧

Nora and Dennis:
Love, Guardian of One's Spirit

This is a story about love—a precious and often too-rare gift with which we mortals struggle. Love can sometimes be pathology, co-dependence, or dysfunction. My relationship with my former husband, Dennis, has been called all of the above. I tend to think of it as something much more profound and simple: love, guardian of one's spirit.

Our story begins like many. We fell passionately in love, and lived and breathed each other—creating home, children, family, and professional life. We modeled perfection, and from the outside looking in, perfection was what others saw. Our life together was simultaneously blissful and horrible. One of the most wonderful blessings was the creation of our most precious gift to each other: our daughters.

Then, after 15 years of marriage, it all came crashing down. The raw devastation of everything we believed in, hoped for, and literally staked our life on was burned to ashes. How could I remain in a loving relationship in a war zone? How could I not vilify and blame him? How could I come to terms emotionally with destruction at my doorstep? I had to find courage and integrity, stand up, dust the ashes off, and realize that my partner was standing in the same ashes. Much more important, I had the responsibility of two very precious children who never took their eyes or ears off me. This sacred and sobering job moved me to rise up and recognize what is truly important. I had to look past the stuff of ego and see Dennis's soul; I learned to allow him to just be. From this place of honoring his essence, conflict dissipated and love could guide.

With this new vision, our fragile and fatigued family still remained sacred territory. We managed to hold fast to our commitment to each other, in a different light, and to our children. We learned to genuinely appreciate what we had to give one another, and continued to engage in a loving and generous relationship. We not only co-parented well, we relied on each other for support, humor, and tenderness.

Toward the end of our sixth year of leading separate lives, I received a phone call telling me that Dennis had fallen off his horse while playing polo and that I must immediately come to the hospital. The scene, embedded graphically in my mind, is one that words cannot adequately describe. I was told that he had sustained a serious head injury and might not live. I then proceeded to do the most painful exercise of my life. I had to bring each child to confront this scene and somehow make sense of this through 12- and 15-year-old eyes. Dennis was in a coma for five weeks before the slow and arduous process of waking up began. It has now been a little over a year. He cannot move or talk. Although he is incapable of performing any physical functions, his cognitive ability still remains, and that has been an important bridge for both of us.

My devotion to this man has only increased. I have washed him, fed him, read to him, and talked to him. As long as both our lives continue, I will do all that I can to make his life as comfortable as I possibly can. I have often been asked, "Why?" Why do I care for a man who is not my husband and to whom I have no obligation? Why, given all the circumstances of our divorce, have I forgiven him? It seems to me that these questions are not so difficult to answer. I think that love is quite simple: When you love so completely that you have forgotten to ask yourself if you are loved in return, you are in the sacred dance.

Among all the things I have learned this past year, the most poignant is that life is fragile and precarious. If I have anything to teach my children, it will be that all we have is our precious relationships, and we honor ourselves and each other by holding fast to our conviction to simply and purely love each other.

chapter 12

My Turn Now

Freedom to Soar

To everything there is a season, a time to every
purpose under heaven.

— Ecclesiastes

In nearly every relationship breakup, there is a time when each person must retreat, take space from the ex-partner, and regain his or her sense of self. Often the pain, confusion, and upset accompanying a breakup become so burdensome that you cannot see yourself or your partner clearly. At this point, the experience of anger, guilt, or fear can be very strong, and any further grappling with the issues of the relationship will only exacerbate your sense of separateness. At such a time, the kindest action you can take on your behalf and that of your partner is to step back, breathe, and do whatever you need to restore your peace, clarity, and in some cases, sanity.

Ideally, it would be wonderful if you could just flow joyfully from one form of your relationship to the next. Some can do this, but most people need time for regrouping. When this time is required, keep it in perspective. You are stepping back not because you hate the jerk and never want to see him again (although that may be exactly how you feel); you are stepping back because you honor yourself and your former partner, and you need to sojourn within to find the love you lost sight of.

The time of personal retreat is a crucial phase in the evolution of your loving relationship. Used properly, it will prepare you for your next step. Used improperly, it will perpetuate or deepen the chasm that makes you feel separate and alone. Such a period is most valuably used as a phase of cleansing and reevaluation during which you consider what has happened in the relationship, take stock of where you are as an individual, gain insight on what you have learned, decide what you want to do differently next time, ask for inner guidance, and reconstitute the emotional integrity that atrophied when you gave your power away to your partner or to fear.

This is also an excellent time to reformulate your vision of your former partner. Consider the huge difference between the way you felt about him or her when you first got together, and how you feel now. At first you may have thought that this was the most wonderful person you had ever met, embodying many or all of the qualities you admired and dreamed of. Remember how open your mind and heart were, how willing you were to overlook their little quirks and foibles (you even thought they were cute), and how much creative energy and generosity you expressed. Remember how the troubles in your life paled in comparison to the well-being you felt with this dear and special person. Remember how wonderful it felt to be in love.

But then *what happened?* How did you stagger so far afield from your original vision? Did your partner change overnight, suddenly shapeshifting from Prince Charming to the Grim Reaper? Or did something inside *you* shift? Did one or both of you become frightened and retreat to an old pattern of self-protection, or did the relationship simply run its course?

Do not stop asking *what happened* until you get an answer that brings you strength and release. Your time of personal renewal is for you to remember the Big Picture, return to Big Love, and use your experience to discover how to generate more rewarding results next time. When you have come to the point where you are willing to accept responsibility for your role in what happened, you will have graduated to the next level of the relationship. Then you are free to be on your own or create a magnificent new relationship, because you recognize that the source of your power is within you, rather than giving it away to whomever comes along.

The clarity you are seeking comes in two realizations about your former partner:

1. *He or she is not God almighty.*
2. *He or she is not the devil.*

Your ex is not perfect, and neither is he evil. You were (are) in a relationship with a human being who has many wonderful qualities, and some that you do not find so wonderful. Welcome to the world! Before you can see your ex (and yourself) clearly, you must take him off the pedestal on which you placed him, and/or remove the "bad guy" hat you set upon him. (It only takes a six-inch fall for a halo to become a noose.) It was *you* who cast him in the role of your choosing (for better or worse). If you were fooled, you fooled yourself (he may have tried to fool you, but if you were foolish enough to agree, you must own the result). And if he was wonderful, it was because you allowed it. This level of creatorship can be challenging to accept, as you may not want to acknowledge that you are responsible for your experience. *But you are.* As a spiritual being, you have been imbued with the power to co-create with God. Everything and everyone who shows up in your world arrives through the invitation of your thoughts and feelings. All experiences are to be enjoyed or learned from. This is how you can bless every person and experience that shows up; they all mirror your own beliefs, and they all serve.

In an intimate relationship, our proclivity to projection is the most intense. If you want to discover what you are laying on the world, just fall in love. Before long, you will encounter every unresolved parental issue, sense of personal inadequacy, and subconscious fear of loss, laid neatly and vividly over the face of your partner. Do not cringe when you realize you have done this, but rejoice. *It is all for your healing*. There is no way you are *not* going to project all over your partner, so you might as well accept the process; and rather than indulge it or deny it, *learn and grow from it*. If you recognize the gift that it is offering, you will be able to purify your mind and heart more quickly and get on with the real fun of discovering who both of you really are, and enjoy your relationship.

Peeling Away Projections

Godly Expectations I Assigned
My Partner

_____

_____

_____

_____

_____

Dark Attributes I Assigned
My Partner

_____

_____

_____

_____

_____

Godly Expectations I Assigned
Myself

_____

_____

_____

_____

_____

Dark Attributes I Assigned Myself

_____

_____

_____

_____

_____

If you can be honest about the projections you assigned to yourself and your partner, you will have made a quantum leap toward understanding your relationship and clearing the way for a more fulfilling relationship next time. Remember that the great healer is *awareness*. Once you bring your shadow to the light, you are free. And you shall be free (in fact, you are free now). The only prerequisite to consistently walking in freedom is telling the truth.

Sample Statements Both Partners Might Make During a Time of Regrouping

From one who needs to step back:

[Name of partner], *I appreciate you and acknowledge you for all the gifts you have brought into my life. I will always honor and care about you. At the moment, I am needing some time to be with myself. Because I want to always see you in the light of love and give you the understanding you deserve, I need to step back and regroup until I regain my clarity. I am not sure how long this process will take, but I trust that it will unfold in the right amount of time. I would appreciate you understanding my feelings and offering me the space to do what I need to do. I hope that you will join me in trusting that this will be helpful for both of us. Please do not contact me until I am ready to communicate with you. I will let you know when that is. In the meantime, I want you to get on with your own life and do what you need to do for your own aliveness, joy, and well-being. I am not throwing you out of my heart; I need this space so I can keep you in it. I know that ultimately we can and will be friends, and I am looking to this time alone to assist me in being able to do this. I wish you well, and I will hold you in my prayers and intentions for good.*

From the other partner:

[Name of partner], *Thank you for your honest and loving communication. I appreciate your need to take time to be with yourself. I would like to remain in touch with you, as I still have feelings for you and care about you a great deal. Yet I want you to be happy, and if you feel that time apart will assist our relationship and ultimately our friendship, then that is what I want you to do. I will think about you and send you kind and loving thoughts as you come home to yourself. I, too, trust that this time will assist both of us, and I look forward to connecting with you again when the time is right.*

These statements are not intended to be a script for you to repeat verbatim or recite without thought or meaning. They are examples of some possible communications—reflecting an attitude—that will move you toward becoming clearer and closer. Amend your own statements to reflect the most honest truth about who and where you are. Speak from your heart.

You or your partner may not, of course, have the clarity to be able to speak these words with full sincerity or intention. You may feel hurt, angry, ripped off, guilty, resentful, or downright stuck or attached. That is fine. These words are intended to offer you a vision of a healthy position to work from. Say as much as you can in the name of peace, and trust.

PITFALLS OF RETREATING

While stepping back to renew yourself is an extremely important process, if you are not clear and pure in your intention, you can misuse the time and ultimately undermine or reverse the goal you are trying to accomplish. Here are a few common pitfalls that may accompany stepping back:

1. Using regrouping as an excuse to run away: If you are hurt or angry at your partner and simply want to get him out of your life, and you have no intention of ever seeing or communicating with him again, you are not regrouping—you are fleeing. The purpose of regrouping is to take care of yourself so that you will be available for real friendship. You have every right to want to get away from your former partner, and if you do not wish to see him or her again, that is fine. Just tell the truth about your intentions. Remember, however, that if you leave with blame or anger, it will prevent you from seeing your next partner clearly. Deal constructively with your upset now, and free yourself from future repetitions of the same issue. Promise yourself that you will not throw your ex out of your heart and that somehow, in some way, you will at least bless him or her from a distance.

2. Taking on another relationship: In the aftermath of a painful relationship, you may be tempted to create another relationship to take the edge off your pain (rebound). Be aware that it is extremely dangerous to fall into love, romance, bed, or be co-dependent with another partner at this time. (Twelve-step programs such as Alcoholics Anonymous ask members not to start a new relationship or make significant life changes during the first year of their recovery.) You want to heal and grow, not repeat. Getting involved with someone else quickly will probably not solve your original hurt, but will compound it. While you may feel an initial rush and exhilaration in being comforted by someone who understands and supports you in ways your former partner did not, it will not be long before your unresolved issues show up louder and stronger. If you have a friendship with a member of the opposite sex and you enjoy talking, then do just that—but leave it at friendship. Do not attempt to begin a new relationship until you feel resolved and complete with the last one.

3. Falling back on an addiction to numb your discomfort:
Earlier, we explored in detail the proclivity to lean on a favorite rubber crutch after a breakup. Use your retreat time to lean *in* on yourself, not *out* on a habit. If you have told yourself, your ex, and your world that you are taking time to renew yourself, and then all you do is watch soap operas and eat bonbons, you are not renewing yourself; you are hiding out. Soap operas and bonbons may be fine for a time if you enjoy them, but in the long run, they are not a substitute for living.

If you are going to take time to regroup, *use the time productively*. Read uplifting books, attend seminars, enjoy meaningful conversations with friends, enter into counseling, spend time outdoors, develop a skill or hobby, meditate, pray, write in your journal, dance, be still, or do whatever nourishes your soul. There is only one criterion by which to evaluate your regrouping time: *Is your inner light growing brighter, or is it dimming*? Of course, you may not feel brighter every minute, and you may have moments where your pain or grief wells up and looms large. Do your best to face and work through these feelings when they arise. Your general trend over a period of time, however, should be toward greater aliveness and wholeness.

The purpose of your retreat is not isolation; it is insulation. You are not going into a black hole to bemoan your sorrow; you are doing your homework to find the light at the end of the tunnel. Rather than shutting down, look within to reconnect with your strength and self-appreciation. You are going into a cocoon to metamorphosize and emerge in a more expanded and enlivened form.

4. Using the retreat as a manipulative tool: If you attempt to get away from your partner in order to make him miss and love you more, you have lost before you've even begun. A real relationship is based on honesty, openness, trust, and clear communication. If you tell your partner good-bye with the unspoken purpose of saying hello again in a week or a month, you will only create more craziness and confusion. If your intention is to end your relationship as you have known it, then have the guts to go ahead and do it. In the long run, it will serve both you and your partner to get on with your lives. Do not say *yes* if you mean *maybe*, or *maybe* if you mean *no*. The clearer you can be with him or her, the clearer you will feel with yourself, and the truth will serve you both.

FANTASY LOVERS

One of the dangers of staying out of touch with your ex is that you may tend to fantasize about him or her, for better or worse. When you do not see someone regularly, you may lose sight of their reality and make up exaggerated stories about their glory or their iniquity. It is easy to a make a human being into a god or devil from a distance. If we stayed with such a person during the course of a real day on Earth, however, we would see them as a whole being, with some attributes that we appreciate and others that we do not.

After a breakup, you may tend to exaggerate the faults of your ex-partner. In the wake of the issues that led to your breakup, there is a good chance that you are harboring residual pain, anger, or resentment. If you do not stay in touch with your ex, you may tend to mentally and emotionally build her into an ogre, remembering all of her horrible attributes and overlooking her noble ones. Permanently and angrily cutting yourself off from your ex will lead you to hold a lop-sided memory of your relationship, which is not fair to the other person or yourself. If you spent some time or had some contact with your former partner once in a while, you would remember her beauty as well as her flaws.

If you are romantic by nature, you may weave a lavish golden memory, overestimate who your partner was and who you were together, and live in an illusion about how divine it was. Of course there were wonderful times, but there were other times—

otherwise you would still be together. I am not suggesting that you discount the value of your partner or your relationship; I am simply inviting you to do a reality check.

Years ago I fell in love with a woman who was not emotionally available, and who mirrored my own fears of intimacy. While my relationship with Donna began on an exciting romantic note, soon a pattern developed that I found very frustrating: Nearly every time that Donna and I had a date, she would break it or show up hours late because she had to drive her children somewhere. After a long period of struggling unsuccessfully to have some quality time together, exacerbated by poor communication skills on both our parts, I recognized that our chances of having a rich and intimate relationship were slim. Donna and I had a long talk, and we said a tearful goodbye.

During the six months that ensued, I could not get Donna off my mind, and I decided that I had missed out on the chance to be with my true soulmate. With the intention of rekindling our relationship, I called Donna and told her that I missed her and wanted to see her. "I really miss you too, and I want to see you," she told me, and we made a date for the next Thursday night. I felt exhilarated to be getting back together with her, and my heart leaped with anticipation.

About 5 P.M. on Thursday afternoon, I received a phone call from Donna. "I'm sorry," she told me, "but I'm not going to be able to make it tonight; I forgot that Joey has a guitar lesson, and I have to take him."

I felt quite disappointed, but after we hung up I felt relieved. I realized that Donna and I were the same people we were when we had broken up, and nothing had substantially changed within either of us to make the relationship different. I was very glad that I had called her, for it helped me to break out of the fantasy in which I had become deluded. At that point, I let go of my hope that Donna was my soulmate, and cleared the way for a more fulfilling relationship.

As a counselor, I have heard some nearly unbelievable stories from people who devoted all their love to someone who was not there. While love and devotion are admirable, they are self-defeating when they are invested in an impossible relationship. I spoke to a woman who fell in love with a monastic priest after meeting him at a weekend retreat she attended at his monastery. When I questioned her about the reality of this romance, she was fully convinced that he was in love with her and that his rejection of her affections meant that he secretly cared about her. She continued to pursue him, and he continued to put her off until he finally ordered her to stop contacting him.

Those with a penchant for romance are blessed with the gifts of vision, passion, and faith. Taken too far, however, romantic vision can be self-deluding; true love, on the other hand, sees clearly and honors the self by pointing us toward true fulfillment, not wishful thinking.

People live in fantasy only when reality is too painful and frightening. If you have been wounded or fear intimacy, it is highly attractive to make up a relationship with someone you subconsciously know will never be there. (Long-distance relationships fall into this category as well.) Then you can enjoy the "benefits" of being in love without having to deal with the challenge of being with a person on a daily basis. Of course the "benefits" do not go very far, since you never really get to be with a partner in a meaningful way. You may have a dream lover, but not a real one. Eventually, if you are serious about creating a real relationship, you will have to face the ways you have deluded yourself, release your fantasy mate, and get on with *building* the relationship of your dreams by showing up and diving into life.

TRANSITIONAL RELATIONSHIPS

Transitional relationships can be helpful or harmful, depending on how complete you are with your last partner and how you approach your new one. A transitional relationship is one in which you get together with someone who feels better than your last partner, but whom you do not see as a long-term partner. A transitional relationship is used as a bridge from where you were to where you want to be. Proceed with wisdom and caution, and write these two words on your mirror: *honesty* and *kindness.*

At worst, a transitional relationship is an abuse of your new partner (and yourself). Grasping for someone on the rebound can cause more trouble than it solves. If you felt wounded or abandoned by your last partner, it is highly tempting to latch onto someone who is more attractive, treats you better, or at least *wants* you. But if you are not truly interested in being with this person, it is unkind to get involved unless you put all your cards on the table. Unless your new partner is in the same position, he may develop deeper feelings for you, and then when you are forced to tell him the truth that you do not see yourself with him in the long run, you will simply take the hurt you incurred and pass it along to him. And so the karma goes on, until someone has the courage to stop the painful cycle by saying, "I will follow my strength rather than loneliness."

At best, a transitional relationship can be a valuable stepping stone. If you have been long steeped in mourning, pain, or guilt, and you have gotten stuck in a self-defeating loop of lonely isolation, such a connection can be a gift to you and your new partner as you open to intimacy, caring, and healthy communication. One of the ways we may defeat ourselves in the aftermath of a broken relationship is to say, "I will not be with anyone unless I know this person is my ultimate life partner." Such a resolution can be helpful if it assists you in establishing new priorities and not wasting your time and energy with partners you don't really like or intend to join with. But your vow can be unhealthy if it leads to cutting yourself off from potentially loving and supportive friends and relationships. You may succeed at screening out undesirable partners, but you may also miss out on rewarding time with quality people.

Sex in a transitional relationship follows the same guidelines—with the stakes multiplied. If you are simply lonely, angry, or horny, and you get together with someone to prove that you are lovable or to get back at the last butthead, you are setting yourself up for more hurt. Falling into bed with someone you do not know or intend to be with is fraught with potential problems. While you might feel good for a moment and compensate for your pain, this other person has feelings—and so do you. Sex has a way of bringing forth our deepest sensitivities and intimacy issues, and unless you are prepared to deal with them, don't poke the snakepit.

It is much healthier to add sex to a relationship with someone you have gotten to know than to become friends with someone in a relationship that has been established in sex.

Take your time and don't go wild immediately. If there is something beautiful and wonderful for you, it will unfold. And if there is not, you will be glad you did not jump the gun.

There is one more potential benefit of a transitional relationship: It may turn into a Big Love. Being with someone on a moment-to-moment basis outside the shadow of overbearing expectations affords you the ease of building a real friendship with a real person. As you drop your image presentation and communicate unpretentiously, you see each other for who you are, not for who you fantasize each other to be. This opens the door to a love that blooms from experience, not glitter. A number of my friends have told me, "There we were one day after knowing each other for a long time, and I looked at him, and all of a sudden I was in love." While I do not suggest that you count on this happening and live on hope alone, I do suggest that you stay open to all possibilities. Sometimes love comes in surprise packages!

A perfect motto for your time of renewal is:

Take good care of yourself.

This is not just kind advice—it is a sort of Zen koan, a thought to be contemplated, a benchmark against which to evaluate your plans and actions. Your time after your breakup is a marvelous opportunity to practice loving yourself. The question to ask when any choice comes before you is, "Which path makes me feel the most alive?" You must bypass your adopted inner critic, editor, and cynic, and listen to the voice of delight that speaks from your heart and resonates through your physical body. Hearken to what your soul says yes to, and don't waste any time with any activities that deaden you. Move with your intuition, and let joy be your compass. The rewards of honoring your spirit will be so great that you will wonder why you ever listened to any other voice. Self-honoring will give you the clarity you missed when you were muddled in the issues of your relationship, and shine the light on how you are to relate now.

"My turn now" calls for great compassion and self-honoring, and certainly great gentleness with yourself. Nobody gets a relationship perfect from the get-go, and most of us spend a lifetime learning about it. Drop any psychic whips with which you have been beating yourself or your partner. Open your heart to the love within you. Then your relationships will be as kind to you as you are to yourself.

∾∾
Jerry and Lexi:
'The One' is Me

My breakup with Lexi really got my attention. It was my second breakup in a year—and I don't even want to tell you what number the breakup was over the last five years. I met so many women I thought would be my soulmate, and the pattern was so consistent: We would meet at a party, at a musical gig where I was performing, or through a friend. I would find myself attracted to the woman physically, and then as we talked, if I liked her energy I would start to feel a "buzz"—a sort of tingly, heady sensation. I swear that each time I felt like I was falling in love—that she was "The One."

There were two things that I had always fantasized I would do with "The One": We would buy a beautiful home together, and we would travel to the Caribbean for a romantic honeymoon. For many years I held off on those two adventures, because ever since I was a boy, I imagined doing them with someone really special.

Back to my pattern: We would start dating and usually fall into bed quickly. I would never date anyone just for sex, but usually I would pick women who, like me, were romantic and sensual, and after a few dates—sometimes a few hours—our connection would get so strong that lovemaking would flow naturally.

Then, after we made love, I would freak out. I would real-ize that I had just gotten involved with someone I did not know very well, and my mind would go crazy, wondering, What have I gotten myself into? *Most of the women I was with became interested in me, and some of them would start planning the wedding—while I was planning my escape. But I wouldn't just leave—I would distance myself emotionally or physically. I would shut down, and the woman would feel it, and she would* start to question me about what was going on—which only made me feel more trapped. I admit that I was not a good communicator—I was just too scared to tell the truth.

Sometimes I would escape into my work (I travel a lot), and the relationship would just peter out over time. Sometimes I would find fault with my partner and make her wrong for something; I would get angry or resentful over insignificant things, and she would leave. No matter the circumstances, the result was the same—the relationship would end, and then I would go on to repeat the story with another woman—different actress, same scene.

After Lexi, I felt such sorrow and frustration over this pattern that something inside me cried, "I can't do this anymore!" I could no longer deny that I had gone over and over the same scenario and that I was creating it. My blaming and excuses no longer convinced me that I was a victim or subject to odd quirks of failed relationships. I admitted to myself that something in me was at the root of what was happening, and the one who needed to change was me.

I felt relieved. I took a deep breath and asked God to show me how to change my way of thinking and living so I could have what I really wanted, and be kinder to myself and any woman who showed up in my life. That felt good; my self-judgments gave way to compassion, and I felt both humbled and empowered. There was hope.

Around that time, I received an invitation to perform at a glamorous hotel in the Virgin Islands. My first instinct was to wonder, Who can I take with me as a partner? But I was not in a relationship, and in my vulnerable state I did not want to take someone just for the sake of taking someone. I wrestled with my lifelong dream of being with my beloved in the Caribbean, and I envisioned feeling lonely and disappointed being in such a beautiful romantic place without a partner. Then I remembered how lonely and disappointed I had felt for so long, being with partners I was afraid to open my heart to.

So I went on the trip anyway, by myself. For that trip, I decided that I would be "The One." Here was a golden opportunity to get to know myself in a way I had not, when I distracted myself with all of these women and the drama that accompanied these relationships. And what peace I felt! I was coming home to myself. I did not need the glamor of being with an attractive woman, or the rush of romance, or the charge of sex to keep me stimulated. I saw how, in many ways, while those adventures were woven with the symbols of intimacy, they were actually distractions *from real intimacy. Real intimacy, I began to see, started with me loving myself for who I am.*

I had a fabulous time in the Virgin Islands. I was more relaxed and present with myself than I had ever been, and I enjoyed my social time with both women and men. Of course I met a few women whom I found attractive, but I did not have the old sense that I had to start a relationship. I had the feeling that I was making friends. My purpose was not to hop into the sack, but merely to keep my heart open and be.

I am writing this on my way back to the airport in St. Thomas. I am going home, but I am not going back to the same home I left. My breakup with Lexi catapulted me into rediscovering myself. Taking this trip by myself was the best move I have ever made.

By the way, I signed the papers on my new house last month. So now I have accomplished my two dreams—the house and the Caribbean—with my beloved. "The One" I have been searching for . . . is me.

Look Who's Stalking

When an Ex Just Won't Quit

*"Surround yourself with only people
who are going to lift you higher."*

— Oprah Winfrey

"The idea of becoming friends with my ex is all well and good," you contend, "but is there ever a situation in which I would be better off to just keep him out of my life?"

Of course there is. If your ex is uncontrollably angry, tipping the scales in neediness, or dangerous in any way, you are better off cutting all ties and doing whatever it takes to free yourself of his influence. If someone is stalking you or could hurt you if you stayed in touch with him, you serve both of you by avoiding situations that could bring you harm.

Every human being is ultimately reachable and capable of creating a rewarding, loving relationship. But if your former partner is not there now, it is not your job to force her to be where she is not. Accept what is, and work from there; true love is ultimately practical, not foolish. Healthy boundaries are a real and necessary tool in building a new life for both of you.

Your former partner wants to love you, and probably does. But if she is at a stage in her evolution where her fear and programming are clouding her ability to see you and your situation clearly, and her actions are toxic to your world, then you must release the desire to have a rational interaction, and connect with her in spirit.

Only you can find the wisdom within yourself to decide if your partner is reachable. Be sure not to cut him off unless you are confident that you have given all the love you can, and he is not receiving it. Most people are able to communicate, if you can just find the right channel on which to connect with them. But if you have exhausted your repertoire of possible channels and you have not gotten worthwhile results, you must let go. Get on with your life, and give him a chance to do the same. He is not dead— just sleeping. Perhaps one day you will be able to enjoy better communication. All you can know for sure is what you need to do now—and that is *all* you really need to know.

Do not fall into the messianic delusion of attempting to rescue your partner from his pain or the mess he appears to be in. If you are tempted to jump in with a life-preserver, most likely that is what you did during your relationship, and you can see where that got you. If your partner is not responding to your good will, it is not your fault. Neither is it your job to make him love and forgive you and speak the perfect words to release you and make everything all right. Your job is to love yourself, tell the truth, respect your former partner's right to choose and learn from his choices, and get on with the business of living fully.

You can sever communication with your ex without throwing her out of your heart. Continue to pray or send loving thoughts in her direction. Hold the vision of her doing well, and picture her in happiness. Play in your mind with the idea of how wonderful it would feel if you could communicate in a rewarding way. Remember that no matter how weird or unruly your partner is acting, she is a whole and innocent spiritual being. If she is engaging in bizarre or unkind acts, recognize that she feels wounded.

Eventually she will have to learn to take responsibility for her experience and take you off the throne or crucifix. In the meantime, you can offer her love and good wishes from a distance.

Keep your own heart and actions pure and effective. Any form of engagement, attack, or retaliation will only delay your healing and push your goal away. Just as you must not let your ex hurt you, neither must you hurt yourself with thoughts of your own powerlessness or victimization. Let your former partner go, place him or her lovingly in the hands of God, give thanks for the gift he or she has been to you, and get on with living the life to which you are called.

~ ~

Toni and Miller:
I Knew This Would Be Best for Both of Us

Even before we were married, Miller showed signs of anger, but I refused to see them—I was in love, and I really wanted to marry him. Over the years, our differences became more and more apparent, and although I wanted my husband to fill the emptiness in my heart, the chasm between us grew only deeper and colder. Miller was distant, wrapped up in work, drugs, and inner rage, and he preferred the bar to coming home at night.

After eight years of dying inside, my soul was breaking down; I was diagnosed with cancer of the cervix and had to have a hysterectomy. Even though I had two beautiful children, this saddened me; I felt that the whole foundation of my femininity was shattered. I was overcome with fear that I would die and be leaving my children. More than anything else at that time, I needed a supportive husband. I longed for Miller's love and understanding, and yearned for him to hold me, to talk to me. But he was so lost in his own sorrow and fear that he pushed me away; he couldn't even give me a word of comfort. When I cried, he got angry and told me to shut up.

Finally, the pain of staying outgrew the risk of leaving. I realized that if I wanted to survive and get healthy, I had to go. Suffering was no longer a virtue. I knew I couldn't do anything to change Miller, and that love was now about setting boundaries. For the last few months we were together, we lived in two different bedrooms and two different worlds. At night, Miller would come into my bedroom, unlock the door, and expect me to "act like his wife." When he started to become physically violent with me, I decided to leave before things got worse. I went to a friend's home and then to the courthouse for a restraining order. I had grown enough to know that this would be for the best for both of us. I knew that love is not letting another person destroy you or himself, and my goal was to create some kind of peace.

A couple of days later, I moved back into the house, and Miller left, with threats of putting a bullet through my brain. Even though he frightened me, I was able to see the situation from a higher perspective. I no longer took his expressions of anger personally—the story didn't fit me any longer. I realized that the things he said sprang from his pain and anger. I felt compassion for him, and all I could do for him was pray and keep myself safe.

Miller continued to vent his rage; he would come to the house and try to open the doors, but I had changed the locks. As he yelled and screamed and threatened me, my heart was beating out of my chest, and my legs were shaking—but I coolly gave him the choice to leave or I would call the police. Somehow he sensed that his words and threats no longer could intimidate me, and he gave up and left.

Sometimes Miller would follow me in his car to check where I was going. One day he sneaked into my bedroom, called me at work, and read my personal journal to me. At times I felt so lost and harassed—it seemed that his actions had no end and that I was his scapegoat. He wanted us out of the house and did everything he could to get us to leave, even withholding money.

I did whatever I could to set boundaries and take care of myself and my children, always keeping calm in order to set a good example for them. I wouldn't speak with him unless he was respectful to me, and sometimes I had to ask him to call me later when he could speak in a civil manner.

Miller had his own lessons to learn. He was stopped one day while driving under the influence and spent the night in jail. He was assigned to county service and group therapy. At that point, he hit bottom. Miller stopped drinking and started to grow spiritually. In time, he learned to face his own pain. He grew more dedicated to our children and respectful to me.

Now, two and a half years later, we have come a long way. We both work together for our children, and our love for them is strong. We are still partners in life in a very important way. Recently he came to help us with the yard. We worked a long time, and then we went to dinner with the kids. As we sat and talked about our lives and our recent dating experiences, his eyes were teary. I hope that someday he finds someone, but now he must get to know himself. I can see his transformation, and we never remind each other about the past. It is mutually forgiven. Love has taken us a long way.

Bring Me a Higher Love

Help from a Greater Hand

"Take God for your spouse and friend and walk with Him continually, and . . . you will learn to love, and the things you must do will work out prosperously for you."
— St. John of the Cross

You may not be able to solve your relationship difficulties by yourself. If what you've been doing until now was working, you would be at peace, and your relationship with your former partner would be a source of continual blessing. If it is, bravo! If not, you are being called to reach beyond what you already know. *A Course in Miracles* advises us, "You cannot be your own guide to miracles, for it is you who made them necessary in the first place." Like all important life ventures, your relationship requires a sense of humility and willingness to accept support. At some point, you might wish to invite a Higher Power into your life to accomplish what you cannot.

What you call this Higher Power and where you locate It is not as important as acknowledging and using It on your behalf. Whether you relate to the absolute God, Jesus, Buddha, Allah, the Great Spirit, nature, Universal Life, the Force, the Divine Mother, the Tao, Infinite Intelligence, angelic presence, your higher self, or simply the energy of pure love, you will help yourself and your partner immensely by opening up to this Higher Power. The whole point is that you are *not* a small person; within you dwells the Power of the Universe and all you need to create positive transformation.

> *Your Higher Power is real, present, powerful,*
> *practical, and available.*

Many people have developed cynicism or resistance to the idea of a relationship with God, largely due to their negative childhood experiences with a church or religion. They may have been taught that God is angry, wrathful, and punitive, and requires suffering and sacrifice from us vile sinners. A significant number of people have found hypocrisy in the church, or religion has turned them off in some way. They may have called out for help to the God they were introduced to by their parents or religion, and not received the answers they hoped to find.

The Higher Power I am suggesting that you contact has nothing to do with the one you were probably taught as a child, and the model of relationships that you were shown has nothing to do with the quality of relationships that you have the capacity to experience.

> *God is love and only love.*
> *The purpose of all relationship is to enjoy love.*
> *God wants both you and your former partner to be happy.*

If you truly wish to create a positive relationship with your former partner, here is a method that will help you above all else:

> *Pray for your ex.*

While this may sound like an outrageous suggestion in the face of all the pain you have felt in this relationship, I suggest that you avoid the temptation to turn the page or burn the book, and read on.

No matter what you have gone through, no matter how much she has hurt you, no matter how guilty you feel for leaving, no matter how much you are fighting or how little you communicate, no matter how much your lawyer is telling you to demand or withhold, no matter how powerless you feel when facing him, yourself, or the world . . .

You have the power to love.

What you are experiencing with your former partner is a result not of what he has done, but of *your thoughts and attitude* about what he has done. You can change your entire experience by elevating your viewpoint. *A Course in Miracles* asks us to remember that "I am not a victim of the world I see" and "I am affected only by my thoughts." Change your thoughts about your relationship, and you will change your relationship.

You have attracted your partner and her actions, for better or worse, according to your thoughts, and you can re-create her—for the better—with your thoughts. Your thoughts were powerful enough to produce a monster, and now you can rechannel the same energy to create a friend. The key to the relationship you want lies not in your actions, but your attitude.

There are several ways you can harness the power of prayer on behalf of your relationship:

1. Send loving thoughts: Take ten minutes daily to generate kind and uplifting thoughts about your partner. Keep your mind focused on her innocence and your appreciation of her. For example:

[Name], *I behold your beauty. I see you as a good and whole person, and I acknowledge the light in you. Thank you for the gifts you have brought to my life. I appreciate you for* [describe several gifts]. *I wish you well in all things. I want you to be happy and successful. I see you in joy and peace. I hope that the things you desire come to you. I bless you, and I honor who you are.*

Continue with positive mental talk for as much of the practice period as you can. It is likely that you will be distracted by negative thoughts or feelings, but do not get discouraged. As soon as you are aware that you have slipped off the beam of love, get back on track.

If you sincerely practice this technique, you will notice several important benefits: (1) You will feel great when you are done; (2) your general attitude about the relationship will improve significantly; (3) you will notice positive changes in your behavior toward each other; and (4) miracles will happen.

2. Positive creative visualization: Get relaxed, set aside any potential distractions, and put on a recording of your favorite soothing music. Take a few deep breaths, and let your mind float into a reverie. In your inner theater, produce a very pleasant movie about how you would like your relationship to be. Envision the two of you talking to each other in kind and gentle tones amidst a scenario of co-creation. Go through all current or potential interactions, such as seeing each other in a social situation or cooperating with respect to child care, and visualize these situations in the way that would be most rewarding to you. Imagine both of you feeling peaceful, mutually supportive, and satisfied with your encounters. Continue until you feel a sense of relief and positivity about your interactions.

Do not use creative visualization to practice voodoo on your partner in order to lure him back into your life, or to force him out of it. The goal is not to try to control his actions, but to lift your thinking and feeling to a level where you will enjoy peace and harmony rather than separateness and strife.

3. Affirmation: An affirmation is a positive statement you take into your subconscious. The subconscious mind is the domain in which we store the beliefs that generate our experience, so we must influence our subconscious before any significant outer change can occur. Suffering is caused by self-defeating thoughts, most of which operate from below the surface of our awareness. You will have no success simply trying to squash negative thoughts; the more you fight them, the bigger they get. But you will have much success by replacing debilitating beliefs with empowering ones. The mind functions like a computer disk—that is, the programs you have written onto it determine the data you output. ("Garbage In, Garbage Out.") If you have a glitch or virus in a program, you must override it with a new and more effective one.

Here are some powerful affirmations you can implement immediately:

The love in me touches the love in you.

My peace I give to you; your peace I now receive.

Love is the only power.

Love is the answer.

I open my heart to the good in our relationship,
and we meet in pure joy.

I release the past and allow the healing power of love
to flow into my life.

I am whole, perfect, and innocent as God created me,
and so are you.

I am free, and I give freedom.

All things are working together for good.

In practicing affirmation, you are not trying to convince yourself of something that is not true; to the contrary, there is a place deep in your heart where you recognize that the idea you are affirming is *already* true. An affirmation does not create; it reminds. It does not fabricate reality; it drills a pipeline through contrary mental mire and taps into the wisdom you already own. Regular practice of affirmation (*gently,* not obtrusively) will yield powerful and long-term effective results. (For further use of affirmation, I recommend all of Louise L. Hay's writings and recordings, especially *You Can Heal Your Life.*[18])

4. Direct prayer: Prayer bypasses the human or personality level of relationship and appeals directly to God for support. Rather than dealing with the store clerk, so to speak, you are calling for the manager to intervene and handle the matter from a higher level of authority. As you lift your thoughts beyond the human dimension and summon the divine, *you must succeed.*

The power of God rushes to support all that is loving.

The form of prayer that you use is far less important than the fact that you are praying. The Great Spirit has a universal translator and understands the intentions of your heart. All sincere prayers are heard and answered according to your willingness to receive the gifts you ask for.

(For a complete overview of the principles of prayer, and techniques that work magnificently, see my book *Handle with Prayer: Harnessing the Power to Make Your Dreams Come Through.*[19])

5. Gratitude: Gratitude is the highest form of prayer. When you dwell in appreciation, you come closest to your divine nature and maximize your power to bring heaven to Earth. Make a list of all the things about your partner for which you are grateful. Include all of his positive attributes, and any little thing he has ever done for you, such as taking out the garbage or cooking your breakfast. Imagine he was on trial for his life, and your testimony on his behalf could save him from the death sentence. What could you say? Each day take five minutes to give thanks for the blessings your former partner has brought to your life. If you cannot find many positive traits, give thanks for the challenges she has brought you, which assisted you in growing. An intimate partner is your best mirror, as she shows you what you love about yourself and what you despise. To discover yourself through her eyes is a gift you could not purchase with all the money in the world. Eventually you will come to a place of appreciation for your relationship. Open to gratitude now, and reap the benefits quickly and forever. (For an inspiring collection of essays on appreciation, read Louise L. Hay's book, *Gratitude: A Way of Life*.[20])

6. Loving service: Acts of kindness move our energy from self-involvement to the delight of giving. Sincere service brings prayer to life. What acts of thoughtfulness could you offer your ex? Could you offer her a little more child care than your divorce agreement calls for? Can you fix her car? Can you buy him a shirt you know he would like, or let him know about a concert by his favorite band? Such thoughtfulness can make all the difference between a relationship simmering in hell and one couched in heaven.

The key element of real service is that it is *unconditional*. If you have a hook attached to the end of your gift and you expect something in return, it is not a gift, but a manipulation. Offer your service purely, with the intent of helping your former partner and bringing more love and light to his life and your relationship. If he doesn't respond overtly, perhaps he is in fear or pain. Assume that somewhere in the depths of his being, he receives your gift. More important, you enjoy the satisfaction of giving from pure love, and you soar beyond the chains of the little self that seeks only for itself. In loving service, you rise to the magnificence you were born to express.

7. Prayer partners: The support of another person or a community magnifies your prayer immensely. If you have a friend who is attuned to the power of prayer or creative visualization, ask them to pray or visualize on your behalf. Tell them that you want help and describe the form of resolution that would bring you relief. If your friend has faith for a positive result in this situation, their confidence will lift you and assist you to put the relationship over the threshold into positive manifestation.

There is a simple yet powerful prayer support system called *Master Minding* [21] (see Endnotes to obtain guidelines) which you can implement easily. Invite several friends to meet with you once a week (over breakfast or lunch, for example), during which you each request and give support for your prayer intentions. *Such a practice can change your life immensely.* You can dissipate nightmares quickly by holding your painful challenges up to the light in the presence of loving beings. (Remember to stay on track and not get bogged down in the details of the difficulty. As soon as you describe the situation you would like healed, immediately turn your focus to the resolution you desire.)

Churches or prayer groups can also be a huge asset to you. Some churches have programs in which prayer practitioners will hold your request in prayer for 30 days or more. While you must humble yourself to ask for help, you empower yourself many times over. If you are not affiliated with a church or prayer group, you may wish to write or call Silent Unity[22] as listed in the Endnotes.

As you align with the power of Spirit, *everything* in your life will change for the better. You will be amazed by the miracles (literally) that will unfold after you have sincerely reached up and out (really *in*) to take hold of a hand larger than your own. Open your mind and heart to a deeper Source, by whatever name (or no name) that you prefer, and you are on your way home. Invite ease to guide your relationship, and you will be amazed at how quickly a battlefield of misery can become a garden of delight.

∾∾

Karl and Thea:
A Greater Hand to Hold

A year after entering college, I met and fell in love with my first wife, Thea. Three years into the marriage, I started getting involved in extramarital sexual encounters and began drinking to mask my shame. During this time, Thea and I were going to a southern Baptist church where I was teaching a couples Sunday School class and serving on numerous church committees. The shame of my double life became too much to bear, and when an opportunity came to move to another city, we took it. I believed that God would forgive my sins only if I would confess and turn away from them, but I knew after four years of trying that I could not quit alcohol or acting out sexually.

Sixteen years later, when Thea asked for a divorce, my question was not "why?" but "why now?" Our separation was friendly because I wanted her back and she knew that I was dealing with issues bigger than I was, and my activities were not directly meant to hurt her. My whole life was coming apart, and without the context of marriage, the only prospects I could see for myself were drinking and sexing myself to death.

After I helped Thea move out of the house, I noticed a magazine she had left behind that had an article in it about sexual addiction. I had never heard the term before, but the moment I saw it I knew that was what I was struggling with. Immediately I began to attend meetings of Sex and Love Addicts Anonymous.

When I discovered that the meetings were held in churches, I was offended, because I had tried the God route and it did not work for me. I was even more discouraged when I realized that 7 of the 12 steps refer to God or a Higher Power. But I was desperate and knew that if the meetings didn't work, I had no hope at all. I did not feel capable of stopping my addictions, but I could commit to going to meetings. I told Thea what was going on and asked if she would come back and help me through the recovery process. She told me that no matter what I did, she could never trust me again, and, at the time, I knew she was right.

After three months of going to meetings and seeing a therapist, I saw minimal results and started to think about suicide. The only thing that stopped me was the realization that if the people in my recovery groups could love and accept me unconditionally, then maybe, if there was a God, He might love me as much or more. Thea had given me a book about God's grace and addiction, in which I read the words, "The heart can respond to the urgings of the Spirit of God while the mind is still trying to figure out what's going on." *This was exactly what I needed. Tears streamed down my face as I prayed to have a real relationship with God. Immediately, a profound peace came over me, and after 16 years of purposely leaving God out of my life, I felt like I was coming home.*

I started an active dialogue with the Spirit within me. I asked if He had some grand plan for my life (like becoming a religious fanatic and going out and preaching to everyone), and He said, "No." I probed, "You have no ulterior motive for talking to me in this way?" Again he replied, "No." Then it dawned on me, "Are you communicating with me this way just because you love me?" He answered, "Yes," and at that moment I fell in love with the Creator of the universe.

Over the months, our love relationship grew, and I came to know, without any doubt, the unconditional love of God. He showed me a vision of me falling down in the dirt, and as soon as I looked up, Jesus was standing over me with his hand outstretched to help me up. Then he dusted me off and said, "Bad spill. Let's keep on walking together; how could I ever leave you when I know I am your only hope of recovery? Together we will grow out of these addictions." After six months of these loving exchanges, He suggested I read A Course in Miracles. *As I started to honor Spirit in all areas of my life, I received the power to do what had eluded me for so many years. It has now been over five years since I stopped my self-destructive behavior.*

I have remained friends with my ex-wife, and I talk to her every few months. The only way I could really make amends to both her and myself is through a changed life.

After my realization of God's presence, I concentrated on my spiritual studies. I was not looking to get into a romantic relationship and was having a good time relating to my fellow students in my classes. Then I met Connie. One afternoon we walked for three hours in the rain, sharing life stories and dreams. I told her about my previous addictive behavior and all the things I was ashamed of. I wanted to get it all out so that if she had a problem handling the information, our relationship would be over quickly. I didn't want any secrets between us—no hidden spots that might come up later and cause a sense of betrayal. She accepted me totally, without reservation, and shared her own hurts and pains. We walked hand in hand over the places where I grew up and talked as if we would always be together.

Four months later, Connie and I were married. Our marriage, now in its fourth year, continues to take me deeper into love and my connection with a Higher Power. Every day we meditate together and read aloud from inspiring books before our daily busyness begins. We share our visions and dreams on a regular basis, re-affirming our purpose for being together in the presence of Spirit.

As I have deepened my relationship with God, myself, and Connie, my relationship with Thea has improved; Connie and I even stayed with her once when we visited Delaware.

I now know that the Spirit of God will reveal Itself to anyone who sincerely asks, and my life is entirely different because I have found a Greater Hand to hold.

chapter 15

Express Way to Your Heart

Can We Talk?

*"There are men [and women] who would quickly love each other
if once they were to speak to each other; for when they spoke
they would discover that their souls had only been separated
by phantoms and delusions."*

— Ernest Hello

"You can imagine my shock when my husband brought home his girlfriend and informed me that she was staying for the weekend," a client told me. "As our divorce began in the aftermath, I remembered that for years I had been bragging to my friends that my husband and I never argued. Then I realized that we also never communicated."

Breakups are gifts because they motivate us to learn from what happened (or didn't happen) in the relationship. Romance has a way of growing trees so thick that we do not realize we were in the forest until we have left it. Life, it is said, is the only course in which the lesson comes *after* the exam.

One of the most valuable ways you can make your breakup work on your behalf is to communicate what you withheld during your relationship. We are only as sick as our secrets, and you can assess the health of your relationship (or lack of it) by how much you have *not* said. As open and honest as we would like to believe we are, usually it is only when the marriage ends that we realize how asleep we were, and how much we denied. As you let go of your expectations and desires for the relationship, suddenly you have nothing to lose, and you are free to tell the truth you hid or postponed.

If, as you are parting, the shift hits the fan, *rejoice.* You have a golden opportunity to clear the withheld material that made you feel a little more lonely and separate each day of your relationship. Your breakup, though messy or uncomfortable at times, is opening more doors for you than it has closed. If you gain the ability to speak more truth, you are better off indeed.

Skills for Communicating with Your Former Partner

1. Center yourself before meeting. Take a few minutes to sit in silence, breathe deeply, walk in the park, or do whatever works for you to connect with peace, clarity, and your Higher Power. If your partner is open to it, sit quietly in meditation or prayer together.

2. Give your partner your full attention. Make plans to meet at a time and place when neither one of you is likely to be distracted.

3. Make "I" statements. ("When you were late picking up Billy, I felt angry," rather than "You made me angry.")

4. Report your significant feelings as soon as possible (while also being sensitive to right timing).

5. "Sandwich" your communication of unpleasant feelings with statements about your partner and your experience that you genuinely

love and appreciate. Begin with your feelings of gratitude, and then, if you wish, discuss issues calling for healing.

6. Avoid reiterating the same statements. If you find yourself repeating something, stop and think about what you can say that makes your message different, more clear, deeper, or stronger.

7. Assume 100 percent responsibility for everything you experienced. Rather than blaming your partner for her shortcomings, seek to discover what it is in you that attracted what happened. By the same token, your partner is 100 percent responsible for everything she experienced. (Read *Conscious Loving* by Gay and Kathlyn Hendricks.[23])

8. Do your best to move the conversation from "what went wrong" or "whose fault it was" to "what we can do now to meet our individual and mutual goals."

9. Do not talk at length about your new lover or relationship, or compare your partner or relationship to another.

10. Ask your former partner, "How can I best support you in having and achieving what you want now?"

THE GIFT OF INTIMACY

As you deepen your communication during or after your breakup, you will feel the intimacy you were missing *in* the relationship. Here you may discover a profound irony: When you withheld saying what you feared would end the relationship, the act of withholding weakened the relationship. Telling your partner the truth about your feelings empowers both of you, as it affirms that you are both big enough to handle the truth, and you trust honesty to work on your behalf. In spite of the old adage, the truth is *not* what hurts—what hurts is *avoiding* the truth.

Since telling more truth restores life force to your relationship, you may find yourselves wanting to get back together. Certainly this is an attractive option; sometimes it takes a breakup to bring a couple closer together. If this is your course, then bravo—your parting has ultimately worked in your favor. If, on the other hand, there is no way you are going to reunite as a couple, your improved communication will serve you immeasurably, no matter what paths you take as individuals.

Deepening your communication will not only help your relationship with your ex; it will improve your ability to create a healthier bond in your next relationship, and all of your relationships. The last thing you want to do is recreate the relationship from hell; if you learn to communicate more effectively, you are ahead of the game, and no matter how bad the relationship was, you have gained a crucial skill. You have transmuted your relationship from a millstone around your neck to a stepping stone to higher ground.

It is never too late to express yourself. In fact, you are not going to feel healed or complete about a difficult relationship *until* you express yourself. Carl Jung noted, "Each of us must tell our story; if we do not, we will go psychotic." In the Gospel of Thomas[24] we are told, "If you do not bring forth what is within you, it will destroy you. If you bring forth what is within you, it will heal you." So speak your truth now and do not waste a moment of precious time. *A Course in Miracles* tells us, "In eternity, delay means nothing, but in time it is tragic."

Honest, loving self-expression is the greatest gift you can offer yourself and those you love. Sometimes what we have to say is not pretty, but the act of speaking from the heart is ultimately healing. I have discovered that if your intention is to create healing, you can find a way to say *anything* that will ultimately bring you closer together. It's not what you say; it's your purpose behind saying it.

The word *intimacy* can be decoded into three words that offer a clue to its attainment: *into me see*. Intimacy is not a gift that just drops down from heaven at your feet; it is an estate you earn by investing the truth—a broader domain you enter when you trust enough to stretch beyond your safety zone. In intimacy we discover the depth of love that was available to us all the time, but which we rarely touched because we feared swimming beyond the shallows.

Real intimacy is not sexual; sexual intimacy is but a reflection of emotional intimacy. You can have sex with one or many partners and still feel lonely, even more isolated than if you were alone. Taking off your clothes does not make you intimate—but taking off your mask *does*. When you are established in your true innocence, you can meet someone, look into their eyes, feel as if you've known them forever, speak words of truth, and experience intimacy deeper than you would know in a thousand sexual encounters.

The truth, it turns out, is not your enemy, but your best friend. It will empower you when all else has failed. Sometimes we turn to the truth only when we have exhausted all other ploys to keep ourselves safe. Yet if you can find the courage and love to speak your truth, no matter how frightening or sordid, the act of sharing it transforms it into a golden gift. Ultimately, the only truth is that we love each other, and all truth-telling is in the service of this noble expression.

Loving Discernment

Is it necessary to tell everyone everything? No. Reporting a particular experience or feeling may create more pain than it solves. Perhaps the person you are telling is not ready to hear it, or you might have to discover a deeper truth within yourself before you bring it into the world. An experience might just be for you, and it would not serve another to hear of it. (Sometimes the best place to speak and explore the truth is with a counselor who can help you get a handle on it before you act on it.) Or, you may have grown significantly since an experience, and reporting it now will only be a distraction to you or the listener.

I spoke to a man who loves his wife and family very much and has a wonderful home life. In confidence, he reported to me that many years ago he had an extramarital affair. When I asked him if he had ever shared this information with his wife or planned to tell her, he answered, "No, I believe that telling her now would only hurt my wife and our marriage. I ended the affair, I learned a great deal from the experience, and I would not repeat it. It is part of my past, not who I am now. This experience is between me and God, and if I am ever supposed to tell my wife, I will know it and do so. Otherwise, it shall remain a personal lesson."

If you are going through a sensitive time in remolding your relationship with your former partner, it may not be the best point at which to dump your dirty laundry on the table. Your optimal path of service depends on the individuals, the context in which communication happens, and the purpose you hold. Like all other decisions, check in with your heart. The most important question to ask is, "What is my motivation?" Are you coming from strength or fear? Are you serving, or just hiding? Do you want to connect, or jab? Try on the feeling of having told the truth, and see what resonates in your heart. This is an excellent opportunity to request help from your Higher Power. Ask for guidance to say the things that will ultimately be in the best interests of both you and your partner, and you will be amazed by the excellent results that unfold.

Telling the truth is more about expressing who *you* are than reporting the details of your journey. Perhaps you know someone who attended a personal growth seminar and came home spouting every detail of their thoughts, feelings, and experience to nearly everyone they meet. But perhaps the office staff doesn't really need to know the details of his latest love/sex interest, and the dental hygienist is not ready to hear why he is afraid of women, or the waitress is not the proper person with whom to discuss the current state of his gastric juices. Indiscriminate truth-telling can be a releasing practice for the speaker, and downright annoying for the listeners!

Sometimes even a few brief, honest words can bring about deep healing and transformation. Telling the truth is about quality, not quantity; real truth-telling creates a magnificent healing resonance. In my seminars, I notice that when someone stands up and speaks honestly from their heart, an energy resonates through the audience like a beautiful chime. Everyone listens with full attention—sometimes the silence is staggering—and a fresh breeze of clarity sweeps through the room and caresses every listener's soul.

What would it take for you to be at peace with yourself and be able to sleep well at night, knowing you have been true to love? The key to successful relationships is to be in integrity with yourself. Perhaps Shakespeare's greatest advice was, "To thine own self be true." Honesty is the crown jewel of self-respect, as it equally blesses the speaker and the recipient.

Visualize a relationship in which hiding has no power to separate you from your beloved. Imagine that no matter how much fear and deception there has been, all of it can be dissolved and transformed with sincere intention to bring forth the higher truth, which ultimately is love. No matter where your former partner stands on his or her path, your own commitment to be authentic will bring you the release and freedom you yearn for. As you make a commitment to bring your relationship into greater light, you pave the way for a new relationship in which dark dreams have no power to distract you from a love that shines far beyond romance, sex, marriage, and the dramas that revolve around them. You are here to discover your true self and live without apology. When you trust honest self-expression to work in your favor, you invite everyone you touch to meet you on higher ground.

∾∾

Chelsea and Ron:
I Took a Deep Breath and Jumped into the Truth

I felt sad when my two-year marriage to Ron ended, but I still kept my heart open to him as a person. Although we had not communicated much since our divorce, my intuition told me that he was holding a grudge; reports from friends confirmed my inner knowing. I did my best to release Ron, but inwardly I hoped that one day we could be close again.

As the years went by, Ron and I both remarried and had children. As destiny would have it, Ron and my husband, Ted, knew each other from business and occasionally talked on the phone.

In early May of 1998, I had a dream in which I was holding Ron and comforting him—he laid his head on my chest, and I put my arms around him. This was not a sexual dream, but one of comfort and nurturing. I woke up feeling happy and hopeful that one day a loving interaction like this might come to pass.

Three weeks later, Ted and I went to Australia's State of Origin rugby game—our version of the Super Bowl. One of the nation's biggest sporting events, this game attracts 110,000 spectators to the Sydney football stadium.

Ted and I had excellent seats for the game—the equivalent of the American 50-yard line. When the game started, all the seats in our section were filled except for one empty seat next to Ted. Five minutes after the game started, a man came and sat down in this seat—it was Ron, my ex-husband. This was incredible, as I stopped to consider that Ron lived in another city 1,000 kilometers away, and that there were 109,999 other seats in the stadium he could have found himself in that night!

Ron, Ted, and I sat and talked, and after a while, Ted volunteered to move so that I could sit next to Ron. In the midst of a huge, screaming, cheering crowd, Ron and I talked about our lives, our spouses, and our children. Ron, the owner of a successful business, revealed that he had decided to simplify his life so he could spend more time with his wife and kids. This had entailed downsizing his company and letting some employees go, which was difficult for him. He said that he would not have been able to meet this challenge without the loving support of his wife.

With two minutes left to go in the game, I took a deep breath and jumped into the truth. I looked into his eyes, told him how glad I was for him that he was happy and how I wished him a future of love. I also apologized for the hurt I had caused him in the past. He held my gaze and said the same words to me, and we shared a meaningful hug.

On the way home, I told Ted what had happened, and he said that even though he could not hear what we were saying amid the frenzied crowd, he could tell that love was emanating from us. I thanked him for supporting me in this forgiveness exchange with Ron. I recalled a line from A Course in Miracles: *"Whenever there is love between two people, there is more love for everyone." I thanked God for a partner who understood this.*

I believe that my dream signaled my intention that I wanted to heal my relationship with Ron, and the universe provided the perfect setting for this to happen. I sit in awe as I consider the miracle of Ron showing up in that one seat, and the depth of healing that occurred against the backdrop of a hundred thousand screaming fans. Even more powerful was the movement within us when we both chose to speak of our feelings in a loving and sup-

portive way. My relationship with Ron has come full circle, and now when I go to sleep at night I feel a new peace in my heart as I give thanks that we spoke openly, and forgave each other and ourselves.

chapter 16

It Takes One to Tango

You Have the Power

"Those who go searching for love only make their own loveless-ness. And the loveless never find love; only the loving find love, and they never have to seek for it."

— D. H. Lawrence

"**B**ut how am I supposed to communicate with a brick wall?" you ask. "My ex won't talk to me, she filed a restraining order against me, and installed call block on her telephone. She's eternally angry at me, but I miss her and want to talk to her. I don't think she ever wants to see or hear from me again."

No problem.

"Excuse me?" you reply.

No problem because of the principle that allows you to heal a relationship no matter what the other person is doing or feeling:

Your experience of your relationship springs from what is happening within you. Get clear with yourself, and you will transform your relationship.

Although your former partner may live as a separate individual who won't receive your communication, she lives within your mind and heart. If you bear hatred or animosity toward her, that energy affects *you*, no matter what she is feeling or doing. And if you generate love and appreciation for her, that is the energy *you* reap. Your purpose after a relationship is the same as in a relationship . . .

Be a love **finder** *rather than a love* **seeker.**

The adventure of love-finding runs far deeper than eliciting a particular response from your partner. The love you seek springs from an inner well, and it does not matter whether you are a mother with four children in the suburbs or a celibate yogi meditating in a cave in the Himalayas.

The most powerful attitude you can adopt is to assume full responsibility for the energy you are putting out now. When you view your partner through the eyes of gratitude, it makes no difference whatsoever what his or her motivations are or were.

Your former partner may be the sweetest angel that ever graced the earth, or the most foul cad to ever debase humanity. He will reap the results of his own choices. In the meantime, you must be cognizant of *your* choices, as well as the thoughts you choose to think. The results you get from a computer are only as good as the operating system you are using to process your data. The facts of your breakup are just that—data. What you do with that information is up to you.

You are entitled to joy, passion, self-expression, and celebration— no matter what choices those around you are making.

Keep the flame of inner passion burning in your soul, and you will reap the unsurpassed pleasure of living in a world of your own bright creation rather than accepting the one handed to you by those who have not yet discovered their own inner beauty.

Ways to Communicate Through a Brick Wall

1. Send a kind greeting card or letter. Do not raise any of the issues of your relationship. Do not ask for anything. Simply offer appreciation, support, and kindness, and indicate that you value your friendship. Assume or expect nothing from your partner. Make your only intention to extend love and express caring.

2. Do not send gifts, flowers, or any items that speak of mani-pulation or require return. Any gift must be utterly free of strings.

3. Do not ask a third party to communicate for you, except to invite your former partner to meet with you if you   both wish.

4. Write your ex a long letter communicating everything you would like to say if he were available to listen and receive your com-munication. Record every wonderful and horrible thought, feel-ing, and experience. Keep going until you feel complete and can't think of or feel anything you have omitted. *Do not send this letter*. This is for your own clearing and resolution. Burn the letter when you are done. Notice the movement you have expe-rienced within yourself.

5. Write a letter to yourself, expressing all of your best qualities, the gifts you gave in the relationship, and how you served your partner.

6. Write the answer to this question: "Why, in wisdom, did I choose this partner to assist me in my own awakening and evolution?"

7. Each day, sit in meditation and devote ten minutes to:

- visualize your former partner in his brightest light. See him as innocent, and hold the image of who he is at his highest.

- do the same for yourself. Love yourself just as you are. Do not berate yourself for mistakes you made, but honor yourself for the gifts you brought to your partner and your relationship.

- imagine your ideal relationship with your former partner as you would like it to be now. Paint a mental picture of yourselves as mutually supportive friends, and feel the harmony you would like to experience.

8. Pray daily for your partner's well-being, your own, and your friendship. Ask the universe to do for you what you cannot do for yourself. Write down your prayer and place the paper in a Bible or other inspirational text, next to a page on which you are promised that prayers are answered.

9. If your former partner requests that you do not contact her, respect her request. Assume that "No" means "No." Be patient. Over time you will heal.

10. Do not speak disparagingly about your partner to others.

THE POWER OF THOUGHT

When I was in my 20s, some friends and I rented a house in the country. Soon after we moved in, we discovered we had an unsympathetic neighbor in Mrs. Ryan, who began to complain about various ways we were offending her and the neighborhood. At the time, diplomacy was not our forte, and we developed a strained relationship with our neighbor. Before long, Mrs. Ryan filed a complaint that our dog was straying onto her property, and our communication ceased.

Then one night I attended a lecture on positive thinking. The instructor suggested that it was possible to heal any relationship by calling the other person to you in your mind and enfolding them in loving thoughts. In the class, we did an exercise in which I mentally pictured Mrs. Ryan before me, and after a few minutes of meditation, I was able to see her in a positive light. I completed the exercise and did not think much about it afterward.

A few days later, one of my housemates ran into the house exclaiming, "You're never gonna believe what just happened! I was out in the garden when Mrs. Ryan came up to me and said, 'I really want to be friends with you. I know that you're nice fellows, and I am sorry if I hassle you. Let's do our best to get along and enjoy each other.'"

I was astonished, as this outreach seemed utterly out of character with the shrew we had come to know. I found it astonishing that there had been no other change in our interaction, except that one evening I sent Mrs. Ryan a few moments of genuine love.

That experience proved to me that . . .

The thoughts, feelings, and energies we generate
go out into the universe, manifest in form, and return to us.

For this reason, we must be vigilant about the thoughts we think, and make use of positive thoughts to beget positive results. This is how you can heal a painful relationship by pointing your thoughts in a new direction. If you hold someone in your mind as a monster, or consider yourself to be the guilty party, you will exacerbate the situation. See the other person and yourself as innocent, however, and the dark history will evaporate, often in miraculous ways.

DEATH IS NO OBSTACLE

If someone dear to you has passed on, you may feel frustrated and incomplete, and wish you had found resolution with them before they left. But you still have an opportunity for healing, since . . .

Your relationship does not depend on physical presence.
Your relationship depends on what is happening in your heart.

My father passed on when I was 18 years old. At the time, our communication was not very good, and I had been disrespectful to him at times throughout my teenage years. Although my father was a good man and a dedicated provider, I did not feel very close to him.

As I matured during the years after he passed, I realized how the distance between us had grown before his death. I began to regret the times I had judged or been unkind to him. In my heart, I wished I could have had an opportunity to express my love and appreciation for him in a way that I was unable to do before he died.

Then one night I had a dream in which I met my father at a party. Although in life my dad had been overweight and not a very fashionable dresser, in this dream he was slim, and attired in a spiffy sharkskin suit. And while he had not been very sociable in life, in this dream he was the life of the party. I approached my dad and told him, "It's great to see you! How are you doing?"

"I'm doing just fine—how are you doing?"

"I'm doing really well, too." I answered.

"That's great!" he replied, and we both went on to mix and mingle with others at the party.

I awoke from the dream with a deep sense of peace and relief in my heart. I felt that I had made contact with my father, and that the separation we had experienced had dissipated. What remained was genuine love and mutual respect. That was a turning point in my relationship with my father; since that time, I have felt much more appreciation for him and greater completion about our relationship.

The fact that my father was no longer alive in physical form did not stop me from restoring the harmony of our relationship. Whether you believe, as I do, that we live in spirit after departing the physical world; or you believe that we simply live in each other's minds and hearts as thoughts and energy, the dynamics and results are the same. As I changed my attitude and intentions toward my father, I arrived at a peaceful resolution with him.

If a former partner has left your immediate world through death or geographical or psychological distance, and it is impossible for you to contact him physically, then you can contact him spiritually. Simply choose a time when you are free of distractions, get into a relaxed position, play some music, take a few breaths, and then mentally call the person unto you in mind and spirit. Take your time, visualize a clear image of the person, and then say to him or her what you would like to say for the purpose of healing or completion. If you do this with concentration and sincere intent, you will be amazed at how effectively this process brings you resolution for your soul.

In the case of a partner who has committed suicide, the surviving partner may feel guilty or responsible for the partner's demise, especially if he left a letter or blamed the survivor. If you are in this position, it is extremely important that you not resonate with the implication of guilt, for this is *not true*. You are responsible for your experience, just as your partner was responsible for his. When you choose to heal the relationship, the cause or circumstances of the death or separation are not important. What is important is your intention to heal it, and your willingness to take internal action to do so.

Here is a sample message that you may say or write to someone who has passed on or moved away from you:

My Dear [Name],
I call you unto me now in the name of love and healing. I know that you live in the heart of God and in my heart. I call you for the purpose of bringing our relationship into the highest light, resolution, and blessing.

I thank you for the gifts that you brought me during our time together. Thank you for [describe gifts].

Now that you have moved on to a new life, I want you to know that I hold you in my heart and wish you well. I know that there were times when we did not get along, and I am willing to let them all go now so that we may both grow and prosper.

I wish you well and bless you on your journey. I release you to go ahead and learn and do the things that your soul needs to do, and I release myself to do the same. I free you, and I free myself. If we are to be in contact, may our communication be based in love and support. I let you go, and I place you lovingly in the hands of Spirit.

This is simply a sample or beginning point for what you want to say. I encourage you to amplify and amend the verbiage so your communication is most meaningful and applicable to your relationship. Some people develop their most intimate relationship with a partner after that person has passed on. I have known several people who communicate with their mate in spirit daily, and enjoy a connection even more rewarding than the one they had when the partner was physically present.

Relationships never end; they just change form. Here we must reiterate the core principle introduced in chapter 1: *Once you are in a relationship with someone, you are in a relationship with that person forever.* You are forever connected with everyone you can remember, as they have a presence in your mind and heart, and they evoke a feeling when you tune in to them. If the notion of being in a relationship with certain people forever tends to generate anxiety within you, take heart. Sooner or later you will transform the way you think about these individuals so that their memory brings you peace. The purpose of your relationship was not what you thought it was; instead, it was a lesson in loving more deeply, seeing more expansively, and discovering a richer beauty in both yourself and your former partner. *A Course in Miracles* teaches, "A happy outcome to all things is sure."

The brick wall you are encountering is just a facade. No one is a brick wall by nature; we have learned to construct walls to shield ourselves from pain. If someone is rigid, they are in pain. Because pain is a reaction to pressure, more pressure will only reinforce the wall. Love, on the other hand, will dissolve walls that pressure cannot budge. When dealing with someone who has erected a brick wall, you must use "x-ray vision." You must see beyond the appearance and recognize that behind the formidable barrier, a sensitive child is cowering. The child doesn't need further attack, but compassion and support.

A seminar participant named Alice tearfully told this story:

Brian was the toughest and most ornery husband you can imagine. Although he was a good provider, he never acknowledged his feelings or responded when I expressed my love for him. Many times I thought about leaving him, but I always convinced myself to stay, and just love him as well as I could.

When Brian died, I went to our safe deposit box to go through our papers. There I found a letter he had left for me:

Dear Alice,

I know that I have been a hard man to live with, and that I have not shown you the affection you longed for. My lack of expressiveness was not because I did not love you; I just didn't know how to show my feelings. Now that I am dying, I want to tell you that I loved you very much, and I appreciate all the kindness and patience you showed me. Thank you for staying with me, supporting me through many years, and being the best wife a man could ask for. You made my life worthwhile.

I love you,
Brian

Don't be fooled by appearances. Remember that . . .

Separateness is the illusion, and love is the reality.

Andy and Debora:
Finding a Common Ground

In 1984, after 13 years of marriage, Debora and I filed for divorce. Our son, Mark, was eight years old. On the surface, the divorce was an amicable one; I even wrote the decree and joint custody agreement, and we had no dispute about property. Below the surface, however, I could not let go of my tremendous feelings of anger and betrayal about the suffering that I felt Debora had inflicted upon me.

In my heart, I knew that the time had come for this unhealthy relationship to move to the next phase of growth for both of us. I knew early in the marriage that Debora and I were on different paths, and we were sharing a brief bit of time together. My struggle was to admit our differences. When we fell in love, it was the ideal of love that we fell for, and not the exploration of life's meaning or our individual purposes for being here.

For five long years after the divorce, any contact I had with Debora was extremely painful, fraught with arguments, threats, suspicion, and covert means of drawing Mark into the fray by asking him to tell each parent what the other was up to. Six months after the divorce, Debora fell in love with another man, moved in with him, and later got married. Secretly, however, I dreamed of reconciling with Debora, and her new marriage only deepened my feelings of separation and failure.

At this point, every event that took place only added to the drama I had created. I played the ultimate martyr, and Mark became the pawn in my carefully strategized chess game to prove who was the more loving parent. I viewed a simple telephone call—over issues such as Mark's school, clothing, health, and what time he was to be picked up—as a criticism of my parenting skills. Even a simple statement such as "Isn't it a wonderful day?" felt like an attack to me. My drama was reinforced by well-intentioned "friends," but others refused to get involved in the public debate I tried to stir up. I resigned myself to the fact that there was no way to ever heal my relationship with Debora.

Then I enrolled in a communications course; I was not particularly thinking about Debora or Mark, but I thought the class could help me in my career. Instead, it led me to a new understanding of communication in all aspects of my life. The key was to take responsibility for listening. I learned that full responsibility for communication rests not with the speaker, but the listener.

One night in class we were asked to think of someone we were having great difficulty communicating with, and with whom we would like to have a breakthrough. Immediately, Debora came to mind. The leader asked if we were willing to create a new "listening" for the person. A new listening—hmm. The instructor explained that if we held a preconceived notion about the speaker, believed that the speaker was less than we were, was always critical, or had nothing to offer us, then true communication and understanding was not possible.

The turning point for me came when the teacher suggested that the most powerful place to listen from is a place where we create a positive prejudgment and find common ground. Suddenly I realized what a huge investment I had in receiving personal approval from Debora; because I always expected criticism from her, I could not hear anything but criticism. In that moment, I decided that no matter what, I would listen to Debora as the loving mother of our son, and no matter what she said, she was saying it from a mother's love for her child.

From that night on, all I heard from Debora was her love for Mark. My emotional charge dissipated, and I responded with the love of a father. Since that all-important decision eight years ago, our friendship—based on mutual love for our child—has grown and flourished in such a way that Mark has been able to feel love from both parents, without having to deal with senseless arguments. Such a simple lesson—letting go of personal attachment, and basing our relationship on God's truth of love.

c h a p t e r   1 7

Is She Better in Bed Than I Was?

When Ex Meets Next

*"Jealousy, that dragon which slays love
under the pretense of keeping it alive."*

— Havelock Ellis

What do you tell your ex about your next? Is it kinder to say nothing or tell everything? Should you all try to be friends, or would it be more prudent to keep history and destiny in separate corners?

The answers to these questions follow behind the answer to one question: *What will work?* What will it take to create the greatest peace, harmony, and empowerment for everyone concerned? What will lead to a win-win-win situation? Here is a promise that will bring you hope and encouragement:

**If you are dedicated to truth and kindness,
you will know exactly what to do.**

The possibilities for the relationship between you, your ex, and your new partner are as varied as the three of you, and your solution to the issues that arise must be custom-tailored to the people involved. One element, however, will be constant: *Love is the answer*.

To discover what will work for you, let's first take a look at what *doesn't* work:

1. Bragging about your new partner: Nothing is more counterproductive than singing the praises of your new partner to your ex. If your former partner is nursing a sense of loss about your relationship, the last thing he wants to hear is how wonderful your new love is and how happy you are with someone who is better than he is. If you engage in any form of comparison, you will likely bruise your ex's self-worth, and he will not hear you objectively. So, do him the courtesy of not rubbing your new life in his face.

Neither will you succeed if you ramble (or drop subtle phrases) about your new partner as a manipulative tool to make your former partner jealous, or to realize how much she really wants and misses you and what a mistake she made to let you go. If you dangle your new "happiness" in front of your ex solely for the purpose of casting yourself in a more tantalizing light, your plan will backfire, and no one will win. By resorting to manipulation rather than honesty, you have fallen prey to smallness, you are misusing your new relationship, and your former partner will be the object of a ploy, rather than loving communication. Don't go there.

If your ex-partner was the one who initiated the breakup, extolling the praises of your new love will probably not stimulate him to want you more, but will actually make him happier. He may find relief that he is "off the hook" as the object of your desire or wrath, and delight in the fact that you have pointed your affections in another direction. I spoke to a fellow who had just returned from the wedding of his former girlfriend. He told me, "People said she was the happiest person in the room—but actually I was."

2. Using your former partner as a therapist: As much as your ex may be willing to support you, she probably does not want to function as your psychiatrist as you encounter difficulties in your new relationship. If you have a lingering emotional tie to your former partner, you may tend to lean on her as you get into painful territory in your next go-round. If you have a good relationship with your ex, she may be there for you—but don't ask her to be a pillow to cry on. You will do better to deal directly with your new partner, and bring the cutting edge of your communication to her. You will grow faster and firmer if you build your muscles *within* your new relationship rather than using your old one as a crutch. Instead of deepening your intimacy with your former partner, seek to develop it with your new one. If you need additional support, go to a counselor or a valued friend. Confine your issues with your ex to your *ex,* and keep your matters with your next lover in that ballpark.

3. Purposely avoiding telling your ex about your new relationship: You may avoid disclosing that you are involved with someone new if you are harboring guilt about leaving your former partner; if you feel you need to protect him from pain; if you fear facing his anger; or if you want to hang on to him and keep him "waiting in the wings" in case you ever want him back. While it is not a good idea to rub your new lover in your old lover's face, neither is it wise to purposely omit him in your discussions with your ex, or make believe you are not seeing someone when you are.

I am not suggesting that you tell your ex about every date or passing interest that comes your way; that is neither necessary nor helpful. But if you get involved with someone who becomes a significant part of your life, then you must inform your former partner. This will serve her in several ways:

- You make it clear that you have moved on, and your interest in continuing or renewing your old relationship is nil.

- You honor your former partner by allowing her to be big enough to handle the fact that you are with someone new. She may not like hearing it, but in telling her, you acknowledge her strength and ability to accept the truth and continue to grow along with you. (The exception, as we have noted, is when your former partner may be dangerous, such as an obsessive clinger or stalker. If someone is irrationally angry or volatile, and your primary intention is to cut all cords, do not discuss your new relationship with your ex.)

- You spare your former partner the pain and embarrassment of hearing about your new love from a third party. Such a roundabout discovery may only add to her sense of separation from you as she wonders, *Why didn't you have the guts and courtesy to tell me directly?*

A variation on not telling your former partner about your new relationship is to play it down when speaking to your ex. You may have informed him about your new love, but if you portray the relationship as less than it is, you are also not being fully honest. Minimizing your feelings about the new relationship is a deception by omission.

One effective method for finding the right communication zone is to imagine, as you are speaking to your ex, that your new partner is listening. What could you say that would communicate the truth to your ex without demeaning your new partner? Use this formula:

Truth equals honesty plus compassion.

4. Indulging your ex's many questions about your new partner: If your former partner feels insecure or competitive, she may delve inappropriately into your new relationship. She may ask, "How was your date last night?" or "Is she a better lover than I was?" or "What do you like about her that you did not find in me?" In such cases, you will do better to give honest yet brief answers that do not invite further discussion. Be open enough to indicate that you are not making a mystery out of your new life, but be curt enough so that you make it clear that you do not wish to go into details. Do not indulge in any comparisons or reveal any intimate issues about the new relationship. If pressed, you may answer, "I do not feel comfortable going into any more detail about my new relationship. Just as I respect the personal issues and intimacy that I shared with you, I want to offer her the same respect." Be gentle yet firm.

5. Creating joint activities with your former partner and your new one: Don't even *think* about creating this type of drama—unless all concerned choose this route.

After my friend Harvey told his wife he was leaving her for her best friend, he tried to arrange social activities in which the three of them could participate. This seemed feasible, as the three had shared many such occasions in the past. For a short time, the scenario seemed to work. Harvey's wife tried to be a good sport and loving person and understand the new couple's relationship. It was not long, however, until the shift hit the fan, and the emotional wounds festered into open hostility.

It was Harvey's guilt about leaving and his fantasy that all could still be friends that inspired him to attempt to merge fire and oil without an explosion. It is extremely rare (*way* to the right on the bell curve) for three people to be able to pull off such a transition quickly and gracefully. In most cases, it would be far wiser to give all the parties space to feel, express, and come to terms with their emotions, than to try to make it all nice immediately. Eventually it *will* be all nice, or at least better; but in the meantime, most people require time to adapt to such a traumatic experience.

Give yourself and your partner ample time for a period of adjustment after a difficult breakup. How long is such a period? That depends on the individuals and the situation. It may be months or years, or your ideal scenario may never manifest as you would like it to. The key word here is *space*. Offer everyone involved the space to deal with the situation in the way that is most healing for them. If you try to force an outcome, you will only experience more animosity and frustration. Allow the person who felt injured to set her own pace and make her decision about if and how much she is willing to be involved with the new couple. Given time and love, each person's spirit will guide them to their right position. Quite possibly, as we have seen in a number of the couples who have told their stories here, you will reconfigure as friends. If not, so be it. Fear forces, while love allows.

Let's summarize some positive strategies to make communication with your former partner more effective and pleasant for everyone:

1. Take everyone's feelings into consideration when deciding what and how much to say.

2. Tell your ex about your next, only to the extent that you provide your ex with reasonable information for her to make her own decisions about how to relate to you.

3. Be honest but succinct.

4. Never use your new relationship as a tool to hurt, tantalize, or make your ex jealous.

5. Honor the integrity of both relationships by keeping the intimate issues of each relationship within their own domain.

6. Do not indulge in your ex's inappropriate questions or fantasies about your new partner.

7. Allow your ex to choose if or how much she wants to be in the presence of you and/or your new partner.

You may remain friends with your former partner, or your paths may lead you in different directions. Your ex may never meet your new beloved, or he might. There is no one way in which these situations are *supposed* to turn out. One principle, however, is certain, and can be trusted above all else: *If you carry love in your heart and ask, in any given moment, "What is required here for the greatest well-being of everyone involved?"* you will know.

We can sum up the entire message of this chapter with one word: *honor.* Honor your former partner for the beauty she embodies and the gifts she brought into your life. Honor your current partner for the aliveness and empowerment you feel with her—as a mirror of who and what you are and where you are going. Honor yourself for making choices in accordance with your heart's desires. Honor everyone with the clearest and highest truth you know.

Rather than punishing yourself for your errors, give yourself some credit for being a test pilot in a cutting-edge technology: *a relationship that works.* History will not remember the errors you made in your experimentation, but will bless you for the master-piece you created.

ᘛᘚ
Ariana and Brian:
My Enemy Became My Friend

When our son was four months old, I found out that my husband had fallen in love with another woman. It didn't help that she was smart, talented, and beautiful. After my initial reaction of anger, jealousy, and betrayal, I realized I had two options: to feel and act like a victim, or to adhere to my philosophy that everything happens for the best and to explore whether my spirit bore some responsibility for orchestrating these events. When I allowed myself to look deep inside, I knew that, while I loved my husband, the relationship hadn't been right for me for quite some time, but I hadn't had the courage to leave it.

While I understood this intellectually, my emotions were in disarray. Again, I recognized two choices before me: to live in hurt and resentment, or to live in love. I shared a son with this man, who would be in my life for at least the next 20 years, if not for the rest of our lives. What type of relationship did I want? I didn't want my son to be put in a position where his father and mother hated each other. There was only one choice for me: I chose love and friendship. This was not an easy choice. It felt like a constant battle—fear or love, fear or love. I had to make this choice over and over again, hundreds of times over the next year, until it became my reality. We opened up communication and talked— all three of us. We shared our feelings. If something came up, we talked about it and cried about it. Eventually, my enemy became my friend.

It is now six years later. My ex-husband is now married to this woman. I'm also remarried, and my ex and his wife live 15 miles away from my husband and me. My ex was my current husband's best man at our wedding, and his new wife was one of my bridesmaids. My new husband and I have a two-year-old daughter and my ex-husband and his wife have a one-year-old daugh-

ter. We share a nanny together, our families have holidays together, we go trick-or-treating together, and we alternate houses for Thanksgiving and Christmas. We've even gone on vacations together. If one of us has an emergency, we call the other family for help. My son loves both his stepparents, and he was surprised to learn that some kids only have one set of parents.

Many people think our relationship is weird. They think it would be more normal if we hated each other! Others tell me how lucky I am to get along with my ex-husband. But I know that luck had nothing to do with it. We consciously chose to have a relationship based on love and friendship. It wasn't easy, but it was important to us. At first, I did it for my son, but in the end, the experience was one of the greatest teachers of my life. We always have two choices: I chose love, and that has made all the difference.

chapter 18

Hello Again

Renewing the Romance

"I am committed to truth, not consistency."
— Mahatma Gandhi

"My mom was married six times, and my father, five times," Marlene told me. "Three of those marriages were to each other."

Marlene parents are examples of why the marriage and divorce businesses have become so lucrative: There are so many repeat customers! Marlene parents showed up at the altar for a total of 11 times between them, and they signed divorce papers 10 times. Like many couples, they said good-bye and then hello again—not at all an unusual occurrence in a world of rapid relationship change.

Even if you have said good-bye to one another for now, at some point you may choose to get together again. Does this mean you were foolish to part in the first place? Not necessarily. If you hit a brick wall and there was no way you could continue to be together as you were, then your decision to say good-bye was wise indeed. Nothing is more repellent to the soul than two people who do not want to be together, yet who force themselves to stay together because of guilt or fear. A true relationship cannot be built on abandoning yourself to please your partner; it springs from realness, communication, and choice.

A seminar participant named Angela told how she had learned about the importance of approaching relationships from a sense of joyful choice. When she and her husband, Ian, got together over 20 years ago, they were well matched and satisfied with their roles. Ian became a respected professional, and Angela devoted herself to mothering and community service activities. Then, after many years, Angela's interests turned to more spiritual activities, while Ian became more involved in making money and ascending the ranks of his profession. Angela became increasingly frustrated with their lack of communication and Ian's unwillingness to participate in the activities she felt were important. Most of their free time revolved around Ian's work and his choice of leisure activities.

Finally, Angela began to see a therapist, whom she told, "I think I could stay in the relationship and be at peace." The counselor thought for a moment, and asked her in response, "But can you stay and be in *joy*?"

What we often call "peace" is simply the absence of war. But there is much more to peace than lack of conflict—just because you are not fighting does not mean you have a good relationship. Dead people do not fight with each other, but that does not mean that their relationship is desirable. Real peace is a sense of joyful fulfillment that wells up within you because you are living true to yourself. Many people resign themselves to feeble relationships with a sense of stoic adaptation, which serves to maintain a certain status quo, but leaves both partners emotionally stuck and stunted. If you try to live without joy for a long time, you miss the whole purpose of living, and your soul begins to shrivel, which is tantamount to psychic death.

A healthy relationship, on the other hand, affords you and your partner a sense of well-being. You are together not because you *have* to be, but because you *choose* to be. While you may experience peaks and valleys within the relationship, your general trend is toward deeper growth, openness, communication, and aliveness. Sometimes your rivers of aliveness run together, and sometimes they run apart. In a strong marriage, these cycles flow within the relationship and ultimately empower the couple. In other relationships, the changes are bigger than the relationship, and the couple eventually moves apart.

So why get together again? There is only one reason to validate the rejoining of a couple: *Both of you have changed.* You are not the same people you were when you were together, and you are not the same people who separated. You have stepped back and reevaluated yourselves, your relationship, and your lives. You have grown, and you are ready to meet your partner at a new plateau with a new perspective.

Unless you have truly undergone an inner transformation, do not attempt to rejoin with your partner. If you do, you will only replay the problems that drove you apart. *"If you always do what you've always done, you'll always get what you've always gotten."* Your relationship will be better only if you have become better as individuals. If you have become more understanding of your partner, more aware that you would like to be with him, more willing to commit your heart, or more forgiving of the negative traits you both bear, only then do you stand a chance of manifesting a better result.

Sometimes time apart increases your appreciation of your partner and smooths out negative thoughts and attitudes that undermined your relationship. A gardener explained to me that gardens in colder climates are in some ways healthier than tropical gardens in a year-long growing season. "When winter comes, many of the harmful bacteria and microorganisms in the soil are killed by the cold temperatures," the gardener explained. "Then, when the spring returns, the soil has been purified, and plants stand a better chance of getting off to a healthier start."

A divorce or separation is like a winter in a relationship; your time apart allows your thoughts, hearts, and souls to be purified. If you choose to come together again, you will bring a richer, more real love to one another. So you can bless your time apart as a gift.

Do not, however, say good-bye with the intention of getting together again. If you do, you will not have a real good-bye, and you will not grow through your separation. If you say good-bye while wishing or planning to join at a later date, your mixed intentions will come back to haunt you. A real good-bye is just that; you are truly letting go and taking a leap of faith into the unknown—and it is only by passing through this initiation that you can discover yourself and free your partner to do the same.

FLYING SOLO

Before you can live in harmony with a mate, you need to feel secure on your own. If the fear of flying solo subconsciously ruled you in your relationship, a period of alone time can help you discover your own wholeness. Then, when you get together with your former partner (or a new one), you will bring forth inner strength and confidence rather than need and co-dependence. Then you can really enjoy your partner and give to her with a whole heart, rather than dancing feverishly to prevent her from leaving.

Sometimes a real good-bye leads to a real hello. My friend Marion spent months in therapy building up the courage to announce to her husband that she was going to leave him. Finally, after much diligent work, Marion confronted her husband with her decision. Subsequently, the couple began to move through the process of separating and divorcing. When I next saw Marion, about a year later, I asked her how things worked out.

"I am very happy," Marion told me.

"So your divorce from Dan worked out well after all?"

"Yes—and no," Marion answered. "I walked through the process of the divorce, all the while feeling sure it was what I wanted. Then, when the divorce papers were put before me to sign, I told my attorney that I wanted a few days before signing them. I went home and meditated, and realized that I really loved Dan and I did not want to leave him. I know it sounds crazy, but going through that whole process actually helped me to recognize how much I appreciated him. We tore up the divorce papers, renewed our marriage vows, and now we are happier than ever!"

If you got together with your partner with sincere intention and later parted in honesty, you were in integrity. And if you should genuinely choose to hook up again, you are still in integrity. Do not be embarrassed about starting over. If you have opened your heart anew and your vision and presence are deeper than they were, you are aligned with your truth—and the universe can ask no more of you. Meanwhile, have compassion for yourself and your partner, and give both of you credit for meeting again on higher ground.

You are a dynamic, evolving being, an expression of life unfolding. We are all making it up as we go along. If you have broken up and reconnected, you are alive. You are in a better position than many couples who stay together for a lifetime, but have died to themselves as they slip into emotionally comatose states. You gain more by parting with passion and reuniting with passion than staying together in a cold, empty shell.

No matter what form your world of relationship takes, the most important thing you can do for yourself and your partner is to *be true to yourself.* If truth takes you apart, you are blessed, and if it brings you together again, life dances through you. It does not matter what other people say or think; all that matters is that you be happy. In the end, the only accounting you need to give is to your own spirit.

ᘒᘒ

Emily and Edward:
What's a Few Divorces Between Friends?

I married Edward in Dusseldorf, Germany, in the winter of 1946. I was 15 years old, a displaced person after being separated from my family during the war. Edward was 21, the son of an Iowa farmer. Soon after we were married, we returned to Iowa to live with Edward's parents and establish our life. Within three years, we had two children and moved, with Edward's parents, to Kansas City, where we bought an old Victorian home.

The next ten years of our marriage were ideal, as my husband's parents watched the children while he began working and I grew up. Things changed, however, when we had seven more children in a row, with the added difficulty of twins dying after a premature birth.

On top of the stress of having so many children, Edward's mother had a stroke and needed to be put in a care facility. Soon Edward's father went into a deep depression. The burden of caring for both parents and children overwhelmed us, with the added onus of Edward having to work as a retail salesman 7 days a week, often 12 hours a day. This left me feeling isolated, lonely, and exhausted. Our problems grew as Edward's parents' health deteriorated. Then his mother died, and two years later, his father, not surprisingly. Edward withdrew further into the emotion-numbing activity of work, while I, in the wake of the loss of his parents (who were marvelous loving surrogates) had an emotional breakdown. Having no means of therapy or outside support, I filed for divorce. I moved out of the house, leaving Edward at home with the kids, who pretty much took care of themselves after school.

I took an apartment and tried to set up an independent life. I had a hard time finding work, however, since I had no trade skills, and I was deafened during the war. Behind all of that, I was very insecure. Edward, who was devastated about the divorce but still loved me very much in spite of my continued rejection, came to my apartment frequently and helped me get comfortable. I began to appreciate the support I felt was lacking during our estrangement, and I realized how much I needed him. With the bonus of no kids underfoot, our affection for each other rekindled, and after a year, we agreed to remarry and start over.

We sold our house, bought another one in an upscale neighborhood, and once again attempted a happy relationship. Everything went well for three more years, and then problems started again. Our kids were becoming teenagers, going out to concerts and dances and having a great time. Meanwhile, Edward continued to work long hours (to pay for the even more expensive house) while I sat at home alone. Soon I was restless and dissatisfied again. Not wanting to miss the party (and being only 40), I went out with the kids—the only problem was, they didn't want me to! Being caught between two worlds and feeling very frustrated, I befriended a few single women my age who were more than happy to recruit me into the singles scene. Within a few months, I asked for a divorce again. This time, since I was enjoying the kids, I asked Edward to move out.

Feeling deeply hurt and betrayed, he moved and we divorced, but he was very angry. This time, rather than helping me when I struggled, he refused. The realities of owning a home and parenting teenagers, some of whom were now heavily into drugs, once again overwhelmed me. And although I was very attractive and tried to create a new relationship with men I dated, I was unable to do so and ended up feeling worse than ever. After a year, I missed Edward and asked him to come home again. After much hesitancy, he agreed but remained distant. We remarried, but we were the same people, and we went along for another 18 months with little real change in our daily dynamics. We needed and relied on each other, but we really didn't have a loving relationship. He still worked; I stayed home and was still unhappy.

When I met a man who flirted with me at a party, our marriage collapsed again. Desperate for attention, I pursued this man to the point of making a fool of myself, and for a third time requested a divorce. This time Edward was furious—he'd had it. He moved out and met a 20-year-old Chinese girl who worked at a restaurant he frequented by himself. To everyone's shock, they moved in together and planned on marrying. I couldn't believe it! All the while I was rejecting him, never in my wildest imagination did I think someone else would be interested in him! For the first time, I felt that I risked losing him forever—a thought I could hardly bear to live with. I worked very hard to convince Edward to give me another chance. At first he wasn't interested, but in spite of our enormous difficulties, he knew he always loved me, and he had to admit that he had neglected me in his efforts to support our family.

Once again we married, and for the first time we decided to seek counseling through our church. This proved to be a good idea. Through prayer, deep communication, and forgiveness, we were able to learn from our mistakes and love one another. Two years ago, we celebrated our 50th anniversary. Ever since we turned our relationship over to God, we have been loving, peaceful, and happy with each other.

At my 50th anniversary celebration, I summed it all up: "So what's a few divorces between friends? It's all a learning curve anyway!" As my children gathered to support us, knowing all the difficulties we had gone through, we stood together as a family and marveled at the healing power of God's grace.

chapter 19

Whatever Works

Models of Success

"The world isn't interested in the storms you encountered,
but whether or not you brought in the ship."

— Raul Armesto

Your relationship with your ex can work, if you want it to. No matter what anguish, turmoil, or outright warfare you have gone through, the moment you value healing more than living in pain, it will come.

A mutually empowering relationship does not require any particular form; indeed, the belief that it is supposed to be a certain way is the source of much unnecessary angst. The only form required is *whatever works*. The methods of healing or redemption of broken relationships are as varied as the individuals who form them. Sandy and Wendell may continue to work together daily in their long-established family business, while Rudy and Ann only see each other every few years at family functions. Melissa will never see Patrick again, but she will send him blessings whenever he comes to mind. Hank and Jessica may discuss the emotional landscape of their new marriages, while Sergio and Ronnie do better to simply restrict their conversation to child care or social news about their friends in common. The adventure of living happily even after (like living happily even before) calls you to discover your own route through. Doing what your friends have done may offer you salvation or spell disaster. One thing is sure, though: The only meaningful question you need to answer and act on is, *"How can we harmonize in order to help each other have what we both want?"*

In this chapter, you will meet five couples who have created unique and innovative ways to support and relate to each other in the aftermath of their separation. Here you will find creative and practical solutions to the dilemma of "how do we relate to each other now?" Perhaps you will find some ideas that you can apply to your situation, but even more important, you will find an *attitude* that will open doors for you.

When your intention is clear, answers appear.

∾ ∾

Cathy and Gary:
I Wish More People Could Believe It Is Possible

After my first date with Gary, I telephoned my mother at 1:30 in the morning to tell her that I had met the man I would marry! We were engaged in the spring two years later while Gary was serving as a Naval Air Intelligence officer in Pensacola, Florida—a situation so similar to the movie An Officer and a Gentleman *that we could have been the lead characters! Just after my graduation that year, we were married at my parents' home in Virginia on a steamy Friday the 13th of June.*

During our eight-and-a-half-year marriage, Gary and I shared many wonderful times, a lengthy trip to Europe, living in five different states, his graduate studies, and finally my emerging maturity. The old cliché, "We just grew apart," pretty much describes what happened. Being a woman of the '70s, I wanted a career, an MBA, and freedom, which meant not having the children he dearly wanted. For three years we talked and talked, had more sad than happy times, and decided that, in the best interests of both of us, we should be divorced. We did not take our decision lightly.

Although it was a heart-wrenching decision, we remained respectful, caring friends throughout the entire process. In August, prior to our final divorce proceedings in November, we went on a vacation to the beach with four of our all-time favorite couples, and we were the only couple who really seemed happy—each of the others had major upsets during the weekend, while we just really enjoyed each other!

When the time came for us to divide our possessions, we opened a bottle of wine, made a list, flipped a coin to see who would choose first, and then we simply alternated until we reached the end of the list. Since both of us wanted our house, we decided that the only fair solution was to sell it and split the proceeds. We also used one attorney to draw up the legal documents since there were absolutely no areas of disagreement. And when the time came to move, we rented one U-Haul and piled in all of our furniture, took his to his new home and mine to my new place, then joined friends for pizza!

Gary agreed to go to court by himself because I knew I would feel too sad to be there—I truly appreciated his strength in doing that. After the divorce, he would babysit our dog, Ralph, whenever I had to travel, and we continued to see each other as friends. Gary admitted that he didn't like being alone, and it didn't take long for him to find a special lady. They were married six months after our divorce was final. Although Gary no longer lives near me, 20 years later we still stay in touch. I will always value our friendship and admire Gary for the wonderful person he is. I wish more people could believe that it is possible to end a marriage and continue to respect and care for each other in the process.

༖ ༖

Patricia and Chuck:
We Started from That Point Forward

After a year of yelling and fighting after the divorce, I looked at Chuck from across a table at the restaurant where we were "hashing out" our differences. We could not seem to agree on any-thing, especially decisions about the care of our daughter, Allyson. I looked Chuck in the eyes and asked him, "Do you love Allyson?"

He resounded with a loud "Of course!"

I told him that I did as well, and that if we really wanted to support our daughter's well-being and get on with our own lives in a healthy way, we needed to get over our differences. Chuck agreed, and we started from that point forward.

We made an agreement that we would not berate each other or attempt to make the other parent look bad, as this would only damage our child's self-worth and teach her negative habits that would affect her future relationships. We decided to love ourselves, forgive each other and ourselves for the past, love our child, and when making decisions about her, to keep love uppermost in our minds and our hearts. We decided to break the cycle of negativity and rise above the pain and hurt. We have really done a good job, and it has made quite a difference in all of our lives.

Here are some ideas we have come up with and implemented:

- *We have monthly dinners together at a restaurant of Allyson's choice.*

- *We set goals with her once a year for the upcoming year, and we plan events together as a family (miniature golf, balloon rides, amusement parks, etc.).*

- *Chuck and I independently deposit money in Allyson's bank account for her future.*

- We mutually agree on bedtimes, discipline, tooth-fairy rewards, allowance, etc.

- Allyson keeps a family picture in her bedroom, a picture of Dad by her bed at Mom's house, and a picture of Mom by her bed at Dad's house.

- We have created a rotating schedule that is best for Allyson's needs, in which the "noncustodial" parent sees her at least three times per week, and both parents have access to her at any time to visit, call, or spend time as needed.

- Both families celebrate her birthdays together.

Based on the success of our experience, I recommend that if you have difficulty working these things out yourself, ask a mutual friend, family member, or counselor to help you establish positive visions and set agreed-upon boundaries. You really can work it out.

∽∽

Bill and Nina:
Call on Me

When we broke up, I was lying on the floor of my office surrounded by my music. After dating for two and a half years, Nina and I knew it was time to end our relationship. We had many great times together, coupled with some extreme lows—the kind that could create deep-seated animosity if we weren't willing to work out our problems. Nina and I started dating other people, but we stayed committed to our friendship.

At the time, I was trying to save enough money to buy my first house, and I found one within my budget. After I made the down payment, paid the closing costs, painted the house, and tore out the 1974 orange shag carpet, I would have a home—and maybe $23 left.

The day I signed the closing papers felt like a miracle. I drove to my new home and basked in the glow of ownership. The next day, my brother and I moved all my furniture and musical equipment in, including computers, guitars, keyboards, and sound boards.

I had been up all night unpacking when the phone rang. It was my Realtor, who had just gotten off the phone with my loan officer. Something had gone wrong! Somebody screwed up. The bottom line on the closing papers was wrong—I was short $4,000! This made my signature, on some 20 pages of real estate psychobabble, invalid. The house was not mine. I was ordered to get out. The seller's Realtor wanted to put it back on the market right away because she knew she could sell it for about $20,000 more because of all the money and work I had already sunk into the house. My Realtor was willing to pay for a moving van, but I wasn't about to leave my house. There was a two-day window for the seller's Realtor to find a new buyer or for me to come up with $4,000.

There are very few people in the world from whom you can borrow large sums of money in an instant. First, of course, they have to have the money. Second, they have to know and trust you on a handshake. I called my parents—they were broke. I called my brother and his wife, who were also broke.

The next morning, I called Nina and asked her for help. She said, "Come on over." I drove to her home, where she wrote me a check for the amount plus some extra spending money because she knew I was broke.

We signed no papers and involved no banks—just two people who were willing to work through the difficult times so that they wouldn't lose a true friend. I paid Nina back four months later.

Nina and I don't see each other much anymore, but I know she will always be my friend and that if I needed her, she would be there, as I would for her.

∾∾

Kim and Peter:
No-Fault Divorce

When Peter and I married in 1972, our intent was to be together forever. Looking back at our childhoods, I realize that we were not given very healthy models of relationship. My father was an alcoholic, and my mother was an enabler. Everything they did was intended to create the appearance of the ideal Leave It to Beaver *family. My parents gave me everything in the material world, but the emotional setting of a healthy family was not there. Peter's childhood was also materially blessed. He lived with a very controlling mother and a co-dependent father. In our marriage, we, too, were very successful in creating an abundant material life; we had been well trained in this curriculum. I also accepted the doctrine that if a woman was to be whole, she had to be married. This is where we began.*

Our marriage went well for eight years until I felt there needed to be something more, and we had a child. This seemed to stir the pot. Peter took little interest in our bundle of joy, and he never changed one diaper. He worked longer hours, and I began to resent his not helping to rear our son. Things began to deteriorate more rapidly. I worked full-time as a teacher, and as a mother I had no time or energy to be a wife, or, even more important, take care of myself. In my heart, something did not feel right, but I rationalized that this was the way it was supposed to be.

In 1986, I went to Russia with a citizen diplomacy group called Teachers for Peace. There I woke up. I saw how things could be different, and I remembered how to laugh and enjoy life—here in this place that I was taught was the evil empire! I stayed with families who ate together, talked to one another, played together, and enjoyed each other's company. They did not have the materialistic stuff we had acquired. On the surface, they appeared poor, but in their relationships they had wealth I had never experienced.

I returned to my home in the north woods of Wisconsin a different person, trying to find out who I really was. This created a great deal of stress in our relationship. Peter repeatedly asked, "When are you coming home?" I had decided to change my way of life, and he did not know the new me. The harder he tried to recreate the old me, the harder I fought to be who I truly was.

When our son, Corey, was eight years old, I went back to the university to study Russian; this forced Peter to be a father two nights a week. We both knew things were not good, and we tried counseling. Two years later, we had an argument that resulted in his leaving, and the following year, we were divorced. In Wisconsin, no-fault divorce is the law. At the time, it certainly did not feel like no-fault. The most devastating thing about the divorce, for me, was giving up the dream of how I wished it to be, and waking up to the truth of how it was. The truth does set one free.

During our separation and divorce, Peter became the perfect dad, and Corey acquired the father he had not had in his early years. Father and son snowmobiled, hunted, fished, and had great times together. Corey lived with me, but he visited his dad every other weekend and for the summer. Peter remarried this past summer. His bride is the wife Peter always wanted me to be, and she is another perfect mom for Corey. I feel truly blessed that they have each other.

Corey is now 17 years old, and this year he is living with his dad. After some turbulent school years, Corey is in a new school in Minnesota, where he's doing well. He is also getting to know his father better. So now he will know both his mom and dad better—what an unexpected gift this is from a divorce! He may even come to understand why his parents were two people who could not live together happily.

Now I truly understand that our divorce was no-fault. I learned through the marriage what I want in a relationship, and I learned through and after the divorce who I truly am. Both Peter and I celebrate our son, and we consider ourselves successful parents; we're just not married. I honor my husband for who he truly is, and I know he honors the person that I am.

Divorce does have its blessings. You cannot change the past, but you can learn from it with love.

✿ ✿
Gina and Randolph:
We Still Save Each Other a Dance

On Labor Day weekend of 1993, I heard a very clear inner voice saying: "Your relationship with Randolph as your husband is over." After two weeks, I sat down with Randolph and shared the message that I had gotten. He was shocked and asked that he have a few days to meditate on the idea. He came back to me three days later and said that he had gotten the same answer.

During the 38 years of our relationship, we experienced a lot of growth, ups and downs, and we moved from being emotionally fused to reclaiming our individuality. This growth helped me remain loving and caring to the man with whom I had spent the largest part of my life. We agreed on many things; the most important was that we chose not to fight during the divorce proceedings. We acknowledged that we'd had many good times, and we did not want to have to think back to an embittered relationship. We had two wonderful grown children and their feelings to consider. We also had a few accumulated assets that needed to be divided in an equal and amicable manner.

Since I'm a professional mediator, I asked Randolph if he would like me to help mediate our divorce. He agreed to my doing the mediation. Randolph and I each went home to our separate computers and made a "draft" of the divorce decree; we then exchanged our documents with each other and edited the documents several times until we came to an agreement. We filled out the necessary legal forms, attached our mediated document, and submitted them to the court to be processed.

We decided that we would continue to live with each other until we could fix up our house and sell it. It took about four months for us to clean and repair the house so that we could get top dollar for it, and another five months to sell the house. We agreed that it was important that we separate slowly, with love and care, so that one or both of us would not get hurt in the process. Many children and adults feel the pain of a divorce so acutely because the partners "rip" the relationship apart, rather than making a clean-cut break. A clean cut heals a lot quicker than a rip.

In our healing process, we each attended individual counseling sessions to help us process our own issues. Our friends and children supported us emotionally through this year-long phase. I also met with a prayer group weekly, where I released any difficult emotional issues to the care of God. I read books on relationships and divorce, and I listened to tapes on healing relationships. I nurtured myself by attending spiritual retreats, getting regular massages, pedicures, and manicures, and getting my hair done. On my bathroom mirror I posted a sign that stated, "I love you." I looked myself in the eye every morning and made that profound statement. Every day after meditating, I stated my affirmation: "I am loving, trusting, confident, fun, and totally outrageous. And I never say or do anything to devalue myself."

It has been almost five years now, and Randolph and I are still good friends. We will always love and care about each other. We occasionally meet to have coffee or lunch. We both love to ballroom dance, and we see each other at our singles dance club and save each other a dance or two.

chapter 20

From Cellmate to Soulmate

Moving Ahead Joyfully

"If you do not get it from yourself, where will you go for it?"
— Buddha

A man sat at the gate of an ancient city, greeting visitors. One morning, a fellow approached and asked the gatekeeper, "What is it like to live in this city?"

"What was it like where you came from?" asked the greeter.

"It was a terrible place," the passerby replied. "Streets were filthy, people were unfriendly, and the economy was so bad I could hardly make a living."

"Well, that's pretty much what you'll find here," answered the gatekeeper.

The visitor shook his head and continued on his way.

An hour later, another man approached the gate; he, too, was interested in moving to this city. "Could you please tell me what it's like to live here?" he inquired.

"What was it like where you came from?" asked the greeter.

"It was a lovely place," answered the visitor. "Great people, nice environment, and I enjoyed working there. It was just time for me to move on; I have the sense that even more is available to me."

"Well, that's pretty much what you'll find here," answered the gatekeeper. The visitor smiled and passed through the gate to his new home.

Relationships are like places we live—islands of consciousness we land on according to what is happening inside of us and the vision we are employing. You will find what you are ready to receive—no more and no less; ultimately the responsibility for what you experience in a relationship rests within your own willingness. No partner is your savior, and no partner is your enemy. Only you can save yourself by recognizing the beauty within you, and only you can hurt yourself by denying it. If you look honestly into your own heart, you will discover that everyone you meet—especially your partner—mirrors your own beliefs.

As I have underscored in many ways, if you expect to have a better relationship with a new partner, you must heal any past relationships that are incomplete. Yet, here I wish to add a grace note:

***A good new relationship can provide you with the support
to find healing with your former partner.***

It is not always necessary that you be fully complete with your ex before you can have a successful new relationship. Indeed, there are many people who move on to new relationships or marriages while still carrying pain, guilt, resentment, or unresolved issues with their former mates. The key to success here is that such individuals open their hearts to love that is bigger than their wound, and love is precisely what heals the wound.

Love is the great healer. In the end . . .

***All lessons and experiences lead to the awareness that
love is all that really matters.***

You may remember the scene at the end of the movie *Ghost*, as Sam (Patrick Swayze) is about to merge into the light. Sam turns to his beloved and declares, "It's amazing—you take all the love with you!" You can practice loving anyone or anything at any time, and *instantly* your love permeates everything in your world. When you are in love, everything is lovable!

If you fall in love with someone new and establish your relationship in real intimacy, you have a strong foundation from which to approach and resolve unhealed issues in your life. If in your last relationship you felt alone, unsupported, and were with someone who wasn't really there, or with whom you did not fully open your heart, and now you find yourself with someone you trust and by whom you feel unconditionally loved and supported, your soul can relax and embrace many truths you could not see when you were afraid and defensive. It is very difficult to see clearly when you feel outside the embrace of love; yet the moment you are again touched by the warmth of that holy flame, you become aware of deeper and richer possibilities that were not obvious when you were struggling.

So it is true that a new love can heal you. Just be careful not to lurch and fall prey to the trap of seeking someone who will fix you, fill you in, or save you. Who you truly are is not broken, empty, or in need of saving.

You are a whole and wondrous being, and as you awaken to your own magnificence, you will attract others who recognize your greatness as well as their own.

When you show up in your full splendor, others show up in theirs.

Relationships, as we have discovered, are not always the way they're portrayed in the movies, in which you meet your beloved, ride off into the sunset, and live happily ever after. In the theaters, that is usually the end of the movie, but in real life, that is just the beginning. A relationship is an epic adventure that calls you to traverse mountains, valleys, streams, and sometimes deserts. It can also be likened to a symphony in which there are sweet caresses of flutes, booming timpani, sweeping passages, heady climaxes, a dance of crescendos and diminuendos, and a whole spectrum of transitions in between. Ultimately you discover that the relationship you thought was between you and another person (or many), exists, more really, *within* you.

Over the course of a lifetime, relationship is a school in which you move from grade to higher grade as you master the lessons of each class. Sometimes you stay with the same learning partner for a lifetime, and sometimes you have several or many different classmates over time; in the end, it does not matter. What matters is that you learn the lessons. Ultimately, all of the lessons revolve around loving more deeply, and as you open to the truth that loving is the only thing that will truly satisfy you, you become freer, lighter, stronger, and happier. No matter what appearances loom in dark moments, everyone is assured of coming home. What route you choose, and how long you travel, is up to you. As the shaman Don Juan told author Carlos Castaneda in *The Teachings of Don Juan*:

> Before you embark on any path, ask the question: Does this path have a heart? If the answer is no, you will know it, and then you must choose another path. . . . On the other hand, a path with heart is easy; it does not make you work at liking it. For me there is only the traveling on any path that may have a heart. There I travel, and the only worthwhile challenge for me is to traverse its full length. And there I travel—looking, looking, breathlessly.[25]

Ultimately, it all comes back to self-love. Self-love is the kindest act in the world, for as you honor your own being, you find the strength, clarity, and energy to give to others in ways you were incapable of when you were denying your own heart's desires. Love yourself first; then, loving others comes easy. Then one day you'll wake up and realize that the jewel you were searching for was not hiding in another; it was in *you*. You had it all the time; you just needed to discover where it was—and use it.

The great promise in the amazing odyssey of relationships is that we go from good to better to best. Nothing in life stays stagnant; if you are not expanding, you are shriveling; if you are not living, you are dying. You are a dynamic being, and love will satisfy you only as you open to embrace more of it daily.

A friend of mine named Alice was feeling frustrated and overwhelmed, so she went to visit her guru and told him of her predicament.

"My child," he told her lovingly, "simplify, simplify, simplify. Get rid of the bad, and keep the good."

Alice went home and made a list of what was working in her life and what was not. Methodically she released what did not bring her joy, and kept what energized her. Her life changed significantly for the better, and her heart came to greater peace.

A year later, Alice again began to feel burdened and less than fully alive. Again she visited her guru and described her experience. "My dear one," the master told her again, "do you not remember what I told you last year? Simplify, simplify, simplify. Let go of the good, and keep the great."

Alice returned to the world she had built, and once again she sorted out her life, this time releasing what was merely good, but not great. She decided she would live only from dignity, and participate in only those activities that she found soul-empowering.

Another year went by, and again Alice felt stuck. She went to her teacher and reported her distress. "My sweet soul," the sage answered, "you have obviously not fully understood my teaching. I want you to go home and really practice now, and do not return with the same question again. Remember: Simplify, simplify, simplify. Let go of the great, and keep only the magnificent."

So, my friend, you have before you the key to healing with your ex and going deeper with your next. Upgrade your relationships—with both ex and next—so that you release what is not working and amplify what is. Do not settle for halfhearted communication or wishy-washy action. Make a stand for how good you can imagine it to be, and invite your partners to step up to the plate with you and claim what is available. And if your ex does not seem receptive, go ahead and live the great life anyway. You serve your ex and your next by living the highest life you know. You inspire more by your actions than your words, and in the end, all you are ever asked is to be true to yourself. Trust integrity, trust truth, trust love, trust God, trust life, trust your heart, and most of all, *trust yourself.* You can and will have your heart's desire.

"To love oneself is the beginning of a lifelong romance."
— Oscar Wilde

Endnotes

1. Kenny and Julia Loggins, *The Unimaginable Life: Lessons Learned on the Path of Love,* Avon, 1998. Music CD and cassette: *The Unimaginable Life,* Columbia, 1997. For an audio cassette of a live workshop on the *Unimaginable Life* presented by Kenny and Julia Loggins, contact Hay House, P.O. Box 5100, Carlsbad, CA 92018-5100 • (800) 654-5126 • www.hayhouse.com.

2. William Least Heat-Moon, *Blue Highways: A Journey into America,* Houghton Mifflin, 1991.

3. *A Course in Miracles: Combined Volume,* Viking, 1996. Supplementary materials available from the Foundation for Inner Peace, P.O. Box 598, Mill Valley, CA 94942.

4. Dr. Gerald Jampolsky, *Love Is Letting Go of Fear,* Celestial Arts, 1988. For information on Attitudinal Healing Centers around the world, founded by Dr. Jampolsky, contact The Center For Attitudinal Healing, 33 Buchanan Dr., Sausalito, CA 94965 • (415) 331-6161 • www.healingcenter.org.

5. Richard Bach, *Illusions: The Adventures of a Reluctant Messiah,* Dell, 1994.

6. See reference to *A Course in Miracles* in note #3.

7. For a listing of Unity Churches, contact the Association of Unity Churches, P.O. Box 610, Lee's Summit, MO 64063 • (816) 524-7414 • www.unity.org.

8. For a listing of Religious Science churches, contact United Church of Religious Science, 3251 West Sixth St., Los Angeles, CA 90020 (213) 388-2181 • www.religiousscience.org or Religious Science International, 1636 West First Ave., Spokane, WA 99204 • (800) 662-1348 • www.rsintl.org.

9. Self-Realization Fellowship, 3880 San Rafael Ave, Los Angeles, CA 90065-3298 • (323) 225-2471 • www.selfrealization.org·

10. Association for Research and Enlightenment, P.O. Box 595, Virginia Beach, VA 23451-0595 • (800) 333-4499 • www.are-cayce.com.

11. For a listing of Dale Carnegie classes in your area, contact the Dale Carnegie main office at 1475 Franklin Ave., Garden City, NY 11530 (800) 231-5800 • www.dale-carnegie.com.

12. For information on 12-step support groups (Sex and Love Addicts Anonymous, Overeaters Anonymous, Alcoholics Anonymous, Narcotics Anonymous, Al-Anon, etc.), consult your local telephone directory.

13. Julia Cameron, *The Artist's Way: A Spiritual Path to Higher Creativity*, J.P. Tarcher, 1992.

14. Richard Bach, *Illusions: The Adventures of a Reluctant Messiah,* Dell, 1994.

15. David and Gay Williamson, *Transformative Rituals: Celebrations for Personal Growth,* Health Communications, 1994.

16. Og Mandino, *Og Mandino's Great Trilogy,* Lifetime Books, 1997.

17. Antoine de Saint-Exupery, *The Little Prince*, Harcourt Brace, 1968.

18. See reference to Hay House in note #2.

19. Alan Cohen, *Handle with Prayer*, Hay House, 1998.

20. Louise L. Hay and Friends, *Gratitude: A Way of Life*, Hay House, 1996.

21. For information about the Master Mind Principle, contact Church of Today, 11200 Eleven Mile Road, Warren, MI 48089 • (810) 758-3050 • www.churchoftoday.com.

22. For prayer assistance from Silent Unity, call (816) 969-2000 or (800) 669-7729, or write Silent Unity, 1901 NW Blue Parkway, Unity Village, MO 64065-0001.

23. Gay Hendricks and Kathlyn Hendricks, *Conscious Loving: The Journey to Co-Commitment.* Bantam, 1992. For information about seminars by Gay and Kathlyn Hendricks, contact the Hendricks Institute, 137 West Mission, Santa Barbara, CA 93101 • (800) 565-1870 • www.hendricks.com.

24. Tom Sannar (editor), *The Gospel of Thomas*, Angel Wisdom Publishing, 1029 N. Jackson, Ste. 1401, Milwaukee, WI 53202 • (414) 272-2645.

25. Carlos Castaneda, *The Teachings of Don Juan: A Yaqui Way of Knowledge*, Pocket Books, 1985.

Recommended Resources

- The Living Enrichment Center and Namaste Retreat Center, 29500 Grahams Ferry Rd., Wilsonville, OR 97070 • (800) 893-1000 • www.lecworld.org. Offers a wealth of services, classes, seminars, retreats, books, and materials, including a weekly cassette tape.

- The teachings of Abraham, through Esther Hicks. Abraham–Hicks, P.O. Box 690070, San Antonio, TX 78269 • (830) 755-2299 • www.abraham-hicks.com.

- Pat Rodegast, *Emmanual's Book*, Bantam, 1987; *Emmanual's Book II*, Bantam, 1989; *Emmanual's Book III*, Bantam, 1994.

- Seminars, books, and tapes by Dr. Barry Vissell and Joyce Vissell, teachers of loving relationship and parenting. The Shared Heart Foundation, P.O. Box 2140, Aptos, CA 95001 • (800) 766-0629 or (408) 684-2299 • bbs.cruzio.com/~sharedhf.

- The teachings of Dr. Carla Gordan and her guides • For information about seminars, books, and tapes, contact Dr. Carla Gordan, 2322 Sawdust Rd., Vienna, VA 22181 • (703) 281-9033 • www.footsteps.com.

Alan Cohen offers inspiring seminars which bring to life the principles of *I Had It All the Time*, and have assisted thousands of appreciative readers to make their dreams come true. If you have been touched by the ideas in this book, consider attending one or more of Alan Cohen's programs:

- An evening or afternoon seminar at a center in your area

- A weekend or week-long retreat at a fine holistic health learning center in a natural setting

- A lecture at an expo, professional conference, or convention

For a free packet of information about Alan Cohen's programs and a current schedule of his upcoming events, contact:

Hay House
PO Box 5100, Carlsbad, CA 92018-5100
1-800-462-3013

The Mastery Training

is a magnificent week in Hawaii which will assist you to remember your soul's purpose and manifest your heart's desires. In a small-group atmosphere offering a high degree of personal attention, you will be empowered and uplifted. This extraordinary seminar offers the paramount combination of a personal growth program and a glorious Hawaiian vacation.

For information about the Mastery Training in Hawaii or to book a presentation at a church, holistic health center, or professional conference, contact:

Alan Cohen Programs
455A Kukuna Road, Haiku, HI 96708
tel: 1-800-568-3079 • fax: (808)572-1023
email: admin@alancohen.com

Visit Alan Cohen's website at:
www.alancohen.com

About the Author

Alan Cohen is the author of 14 popular inspirational books, including the classic *The Dragon Doesn't Live Here Anymore* and the award-winning *A Deep Breath of Life.* James Redfield, author of *The Celestine Prophecy,* calls Alan "the most eloquent spokesman of the heart."Alan's column "From the Heart" appears in many new thought magazines internationally, and he is a contributing writer for the *New York Times* bestselling series, *Chicken Soup for the Soul.*

Alan resides in Maui, Hawaii, where he conducts seminars on spiritual awakening and visionary living. The Mastery Training is a highly focused small-group experience for individuals seeking to bring greater authenticity, love, and integrity to their chosen goals; as well as to add richer aliveness to their work, relationships, and spiritual path. Alan also keynotes and presents seminars at conferences throughout the United States and abroad.

For a free catalog of Alan's books, audiocassettes, and video, or to receive his newsletter including a listing of upcoming seminars in your area, call (800) 462-3013, or write to the Publicity Director at Hay House, Inc., P.O. Box 5100, Carlsbad, CA 92018-5100.

To write to Alan Cohen directly or receive more detailed information about his Mastery Training in Hawaii, write to Alan Cohen Programs, 430 Kukuna Rd., Haiku, HI, 96708; or call (800) 568-3079. Please visit Alan Cohen's Website at **www.alancohen.com.**

Other Hay House Titles of Related Interest

Books

ABSOLUTE HAPPINESS: The Way to a Life of Complete Fulfillment,
by Michael Domeyko Rowland

GRATITUDE: A Way of Life, by Louise L. Hay and Friends

INSPIRATIONS ABOUT LOVE, by Barbara De Angelis, Ph.D.

MAGI ASTROLOGY: The Key to Success in Love and Money

MILLENNIUM 2000: A Positive Approach, by Louise L. Hay and Friends

101 WAYS TO ROMANCE (flip book), by Barbara De Angelis, Ph.D.

PRAYER AND THE FIVE STAGES OF HEALING,
by Ron Roth, Ph.D., with Peter Occhiogrosso

🐾🐾🐾

Audios

*CREATING THE UNIMAGINABLE LIFE: Lessons Learned on the
Path of Love,* by Kenny and Julia Loggins

HOW TO GET WHAT YOU REALLY, REALLY, REALLY, REALLY WANT,
by Dr. Wayne W. Dyer

MAKING RELATIONSHIPS WORK, by Barbara De Angelis, Ph.D.

*OPENING OUR HEARTS TO MEN: Learn to Let Go of Anger, Pain, and
Loneliness and Create a Love That Works,* by Susan Jeffers, Ph.D.

🐾🐾🐾

All of the above titles can be purchased
through your local bookstore, or
call Hay House at **(800) 654-5126.**

We hope you enjoyed this Hay House book. If you would like
to receive a free catalog featuring additional Hay House
books and products, or if you would like information
about the Hay Foundation, please contact:

Hay House, Inc.
P.O. Box 5100
Carlsbad, CA 92018-5100

(760) 431-7695 or **(800) 654-5126**
(760) 431-6948 (fax) or **(800) 650-5115 (fax)**

Please visit the Hay House Website at: **www.hayhouse.com**